Talking Chemistry

What Leaders Should
Know About It

Contact:

✉ christian.m.wegner@web.de

in http://linkedin.com/in/christian-m-wegner-852012123

🐦 http://twitter.com/ChrisWegner99

Bibliografische Information der Deutschen Nationalbibliothek: Die Deutsche Nationalbibliothek verzeichnet diese Publikation in der Deutschen Nationalbibliografie; detaillierte bibliografische Daten sind im Internet über dnb.dnb.de abrufbar.

© 2022 Christian M. Wegner

Herstellung und Verlag: BoD – Books on Demand, Norderstedt

ISBN: 978-3-756-21395-5

🖥 This book is also available in e-book format.

Contents

Talking Chemistry

Personal Note

*"Every special calling in life, if it is to be followed
with success, requires peculiar qualifications of
understanding and soul."*

Carl von Clausewitz, On War, 1832

The motivation for writing *Talking Chemistry* stems from my observation that in today's world of business, 'peculiar qualifications of understanding and soul' do not receive a prominent enough role when people are selected for leadership positions. Therefore, too many managers with little empathy and little talent to motivate people rule organizations, and by not being able to unleash the total potential of their employees, they stand in the way of companies achieving their best possible business performance. It is especially this 'qualification of soul' that distinguishes great leaders from the rest.

The special recognition and appreciation for my work which I have received from my superiors, colleagues, and especially from my employees encouraged me to believe that sharing my experiences by writing this book may be a good idea.

Talking Chemistry is based on the experiences I have gathered in dealing with a large number of companies and organizations, including customers, suppliers, partners, and my 'home' company, for almost four decades of professional activity. Staying interested in business matters even after retirement allowed me some additional and very interesting insights into other companies. These experiences were also a valuable source of inspiration for writing this book.

I am dedicating this book to my parents. From my mother I inherited the joy of writing. From my father I learned that hard work and perseverance are a good recipe for professional accomplishment. Both passed on to me the values of respect and humbleness.

I would like to extend special recognition to three of my former managers who have influenced my career the most. The one who taught me what management is about and trusted me with my first important management assignment. The one who gave me confidence and supported me during the challenging integration process of an additional large business and finally, the one who accompanied me throughout my last years of active professional engagement before my retirement and who introduced the principle: "The CEO is the first servant of his company." Looking back, I realize how great their influence was on me as a person as well as on the development of my career. Especially their trust was extremely motivating for me, and therefore the trust between managers and their employees plays a central role in this book.

I would like to convey my sincere gratitude to my former organization, the international service team of Siemens Logistics, which I had the privilege of working with for more than a decade. Our exceptional accomplishments are still reason for joy and pride.

Finally, I would like to also express my genuine gratefulness toward the Siemens AG which gave me the chance to fulfill my career aspirations. It was my professional home for so many years. Being a 'Siemensianer' was always very important for me.

Thank you, Gert, Cheryl and Daniel, for your valuable support in linguistic matters.

Christian M. Wegner

May, 2022

Talking Chemistry

Preface

Throughout my professional life, I have been fortunate to meet a number of great people who taught me a lot about business and management. I also had the chance to be a manager myself. After I retired, I took inventory of my career, something I guess most people do, and inevitably pondered over the question "What makes a good manager?"

Many top managers—some of whom have even made the cover of business magazines—left behind an incredible mess after taking over initially prosperous businesses. All of them were accredited with a strong personality, insatiable quest for power, and an exceptional capability for making decisions—as such, all the traditional traits of a good manager. So, what went wrong?

If a strong personality ends in narcissism and stands in the way of accepting and appreciating that others are also capable of achieving great results, if the quest for power distracts from the job at hand, and if exaggerated self-confidence leads to wrong decisions, these capabilities no longer have value. To the contrary, such managers become high business risks. Interestingly enough, today's business world still accepts such people in leading positions and gives them a second (and sometimes even a third) chance.

Well, what makes a good manager?

There are a several good qualities that definitely help, such as talent, integrity, resilience, and diligence. Beyond these, I think that genuine trust and humbleness are the two qualities that really make the difference.

Believing in your own strengths emanates the degree of sovereignty required to make others trust in your leadership. But more importantly, you as a leader, trusting your people unleashes the total creative potential of a team. Many managers do not really trust their people and tend to regard them only as business assets who just need to perform. These managers often believe that without coercion and control, employees would rather go for an easy job inside their comfort zone. Some would, no doubt. But in the absence of trust, good employees will not be able to capitalize on their talents and capabilities and will fail to develop their best possible performance.

Trust is a value that needs to be equally shared between managers and their employees. It takes so much to build and so little to destroy. The initiative for building trust has to come from the manager, and there is no easy way to gain it. Too often, managers surround themselves with people known from previous jobs. This bears the risk of perpetuating old customs, structures, and patterns, thus obstructing fresh ideas and suffocating development. Trust needs to be earned, by the managers as well as by the employees. If trust is granted freely and becomes a habit, it can easily turn into a liability.
Facilitated workshops, experience camps, and team events are not appropriate instruments to establish genuine trust. The assumption that freezing together in a wooden hut on a cold winter night or sharing a couple of maggots for lunch in a forest experience fosters bonding and builds trust is erroneous. In such situations, most people will play the role they are expected to play. They will play this role for just a limited period of time (thinking "It's all over after one or two days anyway")

without undergoing a genuine transformation. Most of the results and findings elaborated during and carefully documented at the end of such events will not sustain in real business life. There is no need to create artificial situations to build trust. Daily business yields enough opportunities for that. Genuine trust can only grow in a bilateral relationship between the manager and his or her employees. This can only be achieved by opening up one's own personality and by sharing one's expectations, common values, goals, and individual needs. It is a long process requiring a significant amount of effort. Therefore, genuine trust can only be established with just a few people and should especially encompass a manager's core team. Building a corporate culture based on trust requires flowing this concept from the top level down to the shop floor. Frequent structural changes and reorganizations will strongly impair this process.

Therefore, selecting one's team carefully, trusting good people, praising them, establishing a creative environment for them, and allowing them the opportunity to excel makes a good manager. If granted carefully, trust becomes a tremendous motivator encouraging people to give their very best. Accepting incidental failure is a must and should not affect trust. In a trusted business environment, one's own disappointment in having failed is a far stronger motivator for making it better next time than the fear of consequences.

Humbleness generally has a negative connotation and is often associated with poor or underprivileged people. Some act humble to receive better treatment from their superiors. That is not the kind of humbleness to which I am referring.
Great people are humble even in their greatest moments of success. They are able to recognize and value the contribution

of people surrounding them. Reaching the top, they do not celebrate themselves but rather give exposure to their entire team and use their position to foster the success of young people. Humbleness can allow managers to seek advice or input from their team when faced with difficult decisions. It also helps when dealing with one's own mistakes and failures. It makes it easier to eventually accept being wrong and asking for forgiveness.

Careers of great leaders are undoubtedly the result of talent coupled with hard work. On the other hand, talent and hard work do not necessarily lead to great careers. Favorable circumstances, being at the right time in the right place, a good mentor, and simply luck play an important role in most great business stories. Another facet of humbleness is to accept that occasionally one gets lucky.

Trust and humbleness give mangers a human touch, make them genuine, and enable them to become the top 'servant' of their business. These are the type of leaders most good people want to follow.

Introduction to the Chapters

The first chapter, **The Chemical Factor,** introduces the value of trust. During my entire career, I perceived the trust of my managers as the most motivating factor. In the early days of my professional activity, their trust in my subject matter expertise helped me in solving even the most complex technical problems. Later, the trust of my superiors in my ability to manage a business allowed me a high degree of entrepreneurial freedom and the fulfillment of my professional aspirations. Because working in a trusted environment was so important to me, I invested a lot of effort into earning the trust of my managers—something I strongly recommend especially to everyone who is just starting his or her career: Do not be afraid of taking the first step!

The good chemistry between employees and their managers is of utmost importance for the success of a business. For this reason I decided to start my book with this chapter.

Mutual trust does not just happen; it needs to be earned by the managers as well as by their reports. Because building trust requires a lot of effort, people often shy away from making this investment. This is an observation confirmed by many people from various companies, and therefore, I believe that emphasizing the paramount importance of mutual trust between managers and reports has general relevance. This chapter highlights a couple of aspects about how trust can be established and also addresses some bad practices that destroy trust.

The three following chapters, *The Planning Drama*, *The Race Boat Analogy*, and *The Death Spiral* focus on some important business aspects which, if not properly addressed at management level in due time, can lead to a severe business downturn. Many aspects described in these chapters are based on observations and experiences I made assisting a friend in the recovery attempt of a larger company in the installations business for the automotive industry. Being already retired at that time and thus not any longer active part of a particular business allowed me to have an outside point of view less affected by my own emotions and therefore more objective.

The Planning Drama focuses on the business planning process. This is a mission-critical process because it defines the future development of a business. Thus, it can be well expected that all participants in this process look forward to it with excitement and positive expectations. I have not met many persons who share this feeling. To the contrary, most people hate this period in the business cycle of companies. This phenomenon seems to be common for many organizations, and therefore, I decided to address it. Business planning could be a valuable instrument for aligning everybody toward a common business goal and for strengthening the community inside the company. In some companies, business planning fails to achieve this purpose and therefore should be revised.
Apart from describing general deficiencies of the planning process, this chapter also addresses the shattering effects of bad business planning on companies.

The Race Boat Analogy addresses a common problem at many companies resulting from inflated overhead structures. Even though being the most affected by an unhealthy ratio between productive and non-productive personnel, operational people usually do not openly address such organizational deficiencies. Sometimes because they are too absorbed by the challenges of the daily business. However, the reason often is that staff departments have the stronger lobby inside the company, which is exactly the opposite of what it should be. This chapter shows why the thorough assessment of the added value of functional departments is an important aspect of organizational hygiene and an indispensable management task required to maintain the competitiveness of a company.

Unrealistic business planning and the uncontrolled development of administrative costs were the main reasons for the downturn of my friend's installations company mentioned earlier.

The Death Spiral describes some of the reasons why companies can get caught in a downward swirl potentially ending in a business crash. It addresses some of the possible root causes and analyzes the dynamics of such a potential downturn. Because death spirals, if they occur, usually end in a disaster for all company stakeholders, and especially for their owners and employees, I wrote this chapter with the goal of sensitizing managers to be alert with regard to some aspects that could cause such a situation and of encouraging them to initiate corrective action when it is still time to do so. At the end of the chapter, I am proposing a simple method that can be used by managers to assess the health of their business.

The Ego Trap unmasks managers who put themselves above everything, including the business. In total contrast to such ego-managers, true leaders dedicate all their efforts to serve their company and coach their employees. The rational for this chapter is to unveil the predatory effect of ego-managers on their companies and to encourage organizations to not accept those individuals in leadership positions.

The Value Chimera is a critical debate about the value campaigns of most companies today. By concentrating on a generic level on the company's responsibility toward everybody and everything, these campaigns do not proclaim genuine core values which employees can use as a guideline for their individual actions. Numerous scandals in almost all economic sectors, like the automotive industry and the banking community, just to mention two, demonstrate that individual actions of employees is not governed by the values proclaimed in those companies' value campaigns. This chapter shows where many bad business practices start and also gives some hints with regard to what companies can do to improve their business culture.

The Motivation Matrix is a reflection on what motivates people in business. Generally, managers are only interested if their employees are motivated or not. Very few care about where this motivation stems from. Not all kinds of motivation are equally valuable, and sometimes motivation can easily turn into the opposite and endanger the business. Individual job performance should always be considered in the context of individual motivation. In the second part, this chapter introduces a new method for developing a performance–motivation map of a company, which can be very helpful in defining the best personnel strategies.

The Pentagon Profile is an analysis of different manger types by looking at their attitudes in relation to a broader set of aspects. The method described in this chapter helps elaborating comprehensive and meaningful manger profiles, which can be of great use in the selection process of candidates for leadership positions. It was also my intention to provide managers a guide for working on their leadership profile and to give people some orientation with regard to assessing the leadership qualities of their superiors.

The CXO Dilemma focuses on the business relationship between CEOs and CFOs. In my experience, such a relationship is never straight forward and requires a substantial investment from both sides to be successful. Many CEO–CFO partnerships are not really working well and represent a big burden for the company. This chapter addresses a couple of aspects which need to be observed by both protagonists if they want to be successful as a team.

The Family Business describes how company leaders can achieve that all employees perceive their company as their professional home, and as such dedicate all their best efforts to support the company's goals. The Family Business concept reflects my personal preference for the business setup and culture of a company. Centered around mutual trust and respect, this concept requires a high upfront investment in terms of heart and soul from the side of the managers. For me personally, the image of a manager running his or her business as a 'family head' in a way that all employees feel being part of a great family and perceive the company as their professional home is the most appealing, by far. This is the main message I want to convey to my readers, and therefore, I chose this one as the closing chapter of this book.

Talking Chemistry

The Chemical Factor

Most current management systems rely on structures, hierarchies, processes, rules, and regulations—their purpose being that everybody functions well in his or her role like well-lubricated sprockets in a complex mechanism. They are based on the assumption that if everybody performs their job properly, overall good results can be expected. This is far from the truth! Most people concentrate on conforming and are focusing on their own tasks without caring too much about the overall result. If they can hide behind "It wasn't me," the problem is not relevant any longer, and they expect that somebody else will solve it.

What is missing?

All management systems are built on the interaction between managers and their subordinates. The more complex business decisions are and the more mission-critical individual actions become, the more empathy between managers and their subordinates makes a difference.

"We have concluded an outstandingly successful business year, and I would like to thank everybody for your valuable contributions. But there is no time for relaxation! The upcoming year will also require all of our best efforts. I'm counting on you!"

Talking Chemistry

Have you heard this before? I am sure, you have. It is the gush of regular words most managers throw at their people at the end of the year. Motivating? Not really! As if not every business bore challenges in the past and will continue to do so in the future. Linking praise to a future obligation is a common mistake managers make. Just expressing appreciation often makes managers feel uneasy. Probably because of their concern that their employees may relax and lose their drive. The other reason is that covering praise with a veil of upcoming obligations gives managers the good feeling of not owing their employees. For the employees, it feels like being lifted up a couple of meters for a moment, only to come crashing down shortly after.

So, let us try again.

"We have concluded an outstandingly successful business year, and I would like to thank everybody for your valuable contributions. Let us be proud and enjoy this special moment together. Our success shall give us courage and confidence. We truly are a team of champions, and nothing can stop us!"

How does that sound? Definitively, far better. Everybody would walk away with pride and fresh motivation to tackle the upcoming year. People would feel determined to give their best again. Should there be any special challenges to be mastered in the upcoming year, these could be addressed later.

The above example is just one of many examples why managers do not succeed in establishing good chemistry with their employees. Most of them do not realize how important this *Chemical Factor* really is for their own success and for the success of their business. What does *Chemical Factor* mean in this context? In business, it is the inter-human bonding which ties people together in their joint effort to accomplish a common goal. The foundation of the *Chemical Factor* is built by mutual trust and mutual respect. If present at all, this kind of bonding can be observed more often among peers than between managers and their subordinates.

Mutual trust between managers and their employees is mission-critical for the success of a business. Unfortunately, managers and their employees do not always share this value. To the contrary, deep distrust rules many manager–employee relationships.

During the planning period and budgeting process, when the business goals for the next period are set, mutual distrust between managers and their reports becomes especially evident. Managers are convinced that people want to make it easy for themselves, while people think that managers try to impose unrealistic targets. The problem usually starts with the managers' own targets extending beyond what their teams would consider achievable and fair. Like in a hunting game, the manager (hunter) is determined to skin the rabbit to the bone, while the employees (rabbits) try to sell their fur for as much as possible. Budgeting rounds are often reminiscent of bargaining at an oriental carpet market, as if one could not win without the other to lose. The final goals are far from being mutually accepted, and people will not genuinely feel motivated to achieve them.

For many people, this is the most unpleasant time of the year, and it is usually preceded by much dread for weeks. Beyond frustration about missed targets and potentially lost bonuses, the feeling of being abused and sacrificed by their managers is the most damaging thing for a good manager–employee relationship. What a waste!

So, why do intelligent people accept being put in such a situation? Why do they sometimes even maneuver themselves into it? Of all the possible reasons, some are of an individual's nature, such as pride, hubris, arrogance, or incompetence. Others, such as authority and obedience, are related to today's business culture. But the most critical one is the absence of any real personal risk on the side of most managers. By asking themselves, "If worse comes to worst, what can happen to me?" most mangers would have to answer, "I could lose my bonus." Big deal! That is not a big risk. Some would eventually fear losing their jobs. That is more dramatic, but when taking a closer look, it is not that devastating after all. In the USA, it is not unusual and considered part of business culture to terminate and start jobs frequently. Failing at one job does not really diminish chances of getting another one, possibly even with the prospect of receiving a better paying job. In most Western European countries, labor laws are highly job protective making it quite difficult for companies to terminate underperforming employees. In some countries, terminating a poorly performing employee with twenty or more years of seniority is almost impossible, or it would cost a fortune. Therefore, this person will either be transferred to another position within the company (with the same salary) or receive enough severance pay to be well taken care of for the next couple of years. No doubt, there are also many positive aspects of job security. Feeling safe fosters loyalty toward the company, just to name one. The point is that most mangers do not face any significant personal risk, as opposed to entrepreneurs running their own business and having their own money invested.

Like personal risk, responsibility also is an elusive element when managers eventually fail. Many are ready to immediately claim, "I assume full responsibility!" for whatever goes wrong in their department. This would potentially impress people. "Wow, this guy has guts!" they might think. But is it not a manager's job anyway to assume full responsibility for what is going on in his or her unit? Feeling responsible for one's business should go without saying and materialize beyond words.

Why would somebody refrain from making high promises with the prospect of a rapid professional rise? In the absence of any personal risk and real accountability, there is no reason to do so. And that is why most people are not doing it. "Why would I make it a problem now (by fighting against unrealistic business targets) if it can wait a year (when these targets are missed)?" many managers ask themselves.

With the business targets defined, the focus shifts on daily operation. The best place to start with is a manager's calendar. An incredible succession of meetings, from early morning till late evening, is what can be found in most manager schedules. There are no gaps in between appointments, barely time for lunch breaks, and absolutely no time for any unscheduled interruptions. With such a busy daily schedule, managers cannot find the time to creatively think about their business or to spend with their employees. Most people complain about not being able to contact their managers when they need advice or help. They all have the feeling of being left alone to find solutions to problems while their managers are unavailable.
Staff meetings are often very inefficient. Scheduled regularly and lasting several hours to a full day, they are often a social gathering of business managers and their reports. Most of the time, the attendees work on their own emails or on other

unrelated topics while waiting for their turn to discuss their issues. Because these meetings are usually just a succession of bilateral discussions between the manager and the heads of the different departments, interaction between the latter is often limited to eventually cross-blaming each other. Poor meeting discipline, participants constantly walking in and out, and presenters exceeding their time slots, all make these meetings extremely inefficient and a big waste of time.

Another negative aspect about large scale meetings is that they are often abused to socialize responsibility. Whenever somebody wants to avoid the personal accountability for a problem or to get around solving it on his or her own, a meeting is organized. Many people believe that once their managers are made aware, an issue immediately loses its criticality. "As already addressed in staff meeting xyz, …," the issue suddenly becomes everybody's problem, including management's. Many managers make the mistake of tolerating such an attitude. As a result, other meetings are set up to control the problem, additional support is appointed, and the original responsibility gets totally diluted. Most of these meetings end with everybody leaving with the impression of having wasted their time. Even though most staff meetings are inefficient, managers still love them and would not change a thing.

Calling for all these meetings makes managers believe they have the organization under control and having paid enough tribute to the necessity of communicating with their employees. They fail to understand that meetings are not a substitute for individual interaction with their people.

Generally, this meeting hysteria obstructs fluent communication and personal interaction in the company. People need to set up meetings well in advance if they want to discuss something with their managers. Getting an appointment with one's manager often becomes a difficult task requiring a lot of tenacity and perseverance. Trapped in this meeting avalanche, people find it more and more difficult to effectively manage their work according to their own work style and personal preferences. Increasingly driven from the outside, they feel like business assets rather than as valued individuals. For them, managers become something remote and inaccessible.

Another demotivating effect resulting from overloaded manager schedules is letting people sit and wait or postponing meetings at the last minute. Comprehensive preparation and extensive travel are often required when people go into a management meeting. Thus, it is a matter of respect that managers give their reports their undivided attention. But often this is not the case. How often do people have the impression of talking to the wall, while their managers are absorbed by other things?

To be efficient, meetings should be organized in a way that they require the active engagement of all participants. This means selecting the right topics and inviting the right people to discuss them. Bilateral issues should be addressed on a bilateral level, and non-involved parties should not be present.
Managers should also regard these meetings as valuable instruments to get people aligned. They should use them to foster co-operation, bring people together, and especially to improve the bonding between themselves and their reports. To succeed, meetings require good preparation, intensive participation, and a lot of after-meeting work. Therefore, their number must be reduced.

Managers should ask themselves, "Do I really need to set up all these meetings burning up all my time? Most are not very productive anyway. What would happen if I canceled some of them?" People would start acting more independently, feel more responsible, and show up better prepared.

Managers should invest some time into assessing the communication culture in their departments or companies. Does the 'need to know' principle prevail, or does everybody get informed about everything? Do people put their heads together by their own initiative when a problem arises, or do they wait for their manager to set up a meeting?

Once, a fellow manager and friend asked me what kind of advice I could give him regarding the relationship with his people. "Declutter your calendar and spend more time on direct and individual interaction with your employees. It is all about improving the chemistry between you and your people," was my answer. Managers should smartly balance their time between regular meetings, their flexible availability for direct interaction with their people, and for thinking about their business. The freedom to close the office door every now and then letting the mind roam for a couple of minutes is the perfect germination ground for best business ideas. Inviting employees (and not necessarily only the direct reports) in for a short chat outside the regular meeting schedule, asking what they think about the business, offering help if needed, and eventually also talking about things beyond the job will take the manager–employee relationship to a superior level.

In conclusion, what could be the common denominator for people to drive them toward professional excellence? What will make them give their best? We have seen, it is not professional risk, and it is not accountability toward their superiors either. Money? Maybe, but it will not last. Any raise will be taken for granted shortly after and lose its motivating effect. A promotion? Probably, but there is only a limited number of individuals that can be promoted. What about all the others?

In my view, the personal push employees feel by perceiving the company as their professional home is what makes them excel. Rather than seeing the company as an instrument for fulfilling a personal career plan, managers must take on ownership of their business. Not material ownership, because the company belongs to somebody else. Instead, it is the moral ownership of the companies they serve. As this kind of ownership resides in the hearts and souls of people, not everybody is capable of developing such a feeling and of embracing such an attitude. Therefore, not everybody can become an excellent manager. Companies must strive to become good professional homes for their people, and it is the job of the managers to make it happen. Leading people, and that is what in most cases managing a business is about, means finding one's way into their hearts and souls, making them feel a moral obligation toward the company, and making them want to do a job well.

In the sixties and seventies, more companies succeeded in implementing such a business culture. Today, as a tribute to a new management style, it unfortunately became increasingly unfashionable. Instead of trust and personal motivation, distrust, fear, and obedience became the prevailing elements of today's management culture. And therefore, many businesses remain far below their potential.

A positive business culture based on trust and co-operation is one of the most valuable company assets. Implementing it requires a strong commitment from the top, perseverance, and a lot of time. Business leaders should not shy away from dedicating their best effort toward this goal.

The Planning Drama

The planning process defines the strategies, sets the targets, and determines the resources for the future development of a business. Thus, planning is an essential instrument of business management. A sound and realistic business plan is an important success factor because it directs all business means and efforts. Inconsistent and unrealistic business plans not only waste a company's resources, they can even put the whole business in jeopardy.

<<<<< >>>>>

It is quite astonishing how little management attention is often allocated to the consistency of the planning process. What is also surprising is how unprofessionally business plans are sometimes made.

In the following, two important systematic reasons for poor business planning will be addressed.

Business strategies and targets are often defined by top management and then flowed down within the organization without an appropriate feedback loop from the bottom up.

Instead of entering into a dialogue with their different business units to jointly determine the direction of the business, managers often set targets that cannot be achieved or lead the business in the wrong direction. "We don't discuss targets, we may just eventually discuss ways of achieving them," is a common statement made by managers in the attempt to demonstrate authority. Beyond vague ideas with no practical relevance, in most cases, they do not really have in mind a concrete path of how to achieve these targets. "I provided you with a compass, now don't expect me to also walk you out of the woods," is another killer phrase often heard in this context. Doubt of achieving set business targets is generally not accepted and considered a weakness. Therefore, being afraid of displeasing their bosses, many managers choose the path of least resistance by agreeing to business targets that they know will not be achievable. Smart people will try to keep an escape door open for themselves by linking target fulfillment to boundary conditions. When eventually the targets are not met, they will concentrate all their efforts on finding excuses and blaming the outcome on unfavorable circumstances beyond their control. Of course, this bad system kills all entrepreneurial spirit, as people focus more on dealing with the consequences of failure rather than on the business itself.

Fearing their superiors, business managers often flow down, without further reflection, unattainable business expectations within their organization. Planning meetings typically take the form of an odd battle between the managers and their groups. Even though managers may not be convinced about their targets themselves, they will still try to impose them on their people.

As an example, assuming that a manager's target is 100, he or she would usually insist on individual team targets aggregating to more than 100, regardless of feasibility. This would give him or her a safety margin for reaching his or her own goals. Stereotype phrases such as "We would have expected a higher ambition from you and your team" or "You should demonstrate a more challenging commitment" are too easily used on people. These kind of statements imply that people have no drive and no high ambitions. They are insulting and demotivating. This approach often results in unrealistic business expectations, with no one believing in their targets or in the ability of their managers.

With every manager having his or her own manager, this awkward process sometimes generates a pyramid of false expectations and promises. This pyramid is bound to collapse at the end of the business year when the results sometimes substantially deviate from the original targets.

Managers seldom have the courage to argue with their superiors about business targets. Business meetings joined by a manager, his or her team, and the manager's superiors are often quite bizarre. The correct approach would be for managers to align the meeting contents and strategy first with their team and then jointly sustain their conclusions to their superiors. This would be a good opportunity to demonstrate their commitment toward their people. But too often, these meetings end up in a bashing where managers sometimes even ally with their superiors against their own teams instead of fulfilling their duty to protect them.

How do we overcome this mess? A good start would be for every manager to first sit down with his or her closest employees to explore what can be realistically accomplished and to determine what would be the comfort zone, what is a reasonable challenge, and where it becomes critical. Past performance could be a good reference, but an outstanding last year should not automatically turn into an obligation for the next one. This would make people feel they are being punished for their achievements.

Talking Chemistry

Returning to our prior example, it could be assumed that after a joint assessment, the manager and his or her team agree that 80 would be quite easily achieved. This is the comfort zone. It would be the absolute low-water mark, while an additional 10 could be a fair challenge supported by valid arguments from both sides. So, what about the open gap of 10 to get to 100? Believing in the capabilities of his or her teams and the feasibility of the 100 target, a smart manager would take this gap as a personal challenge, putting his or her own neck on the chopping block. Without believing in this target, it would be professionally unethical to accept it. Properly communicated, this approach would strongly contribute to a better bonding between managers and their employees. Most people would feel solidarity with their manager and voluntarily go the extra mile to achieve the remaining 10.

Managers often start a new assignment without having the required specific expertise for the new job. This could be, for example, the case when new managers are hired from outside the company or when managers are moved from one business line to another inside larger corporations.

Technical businesses are very different from each other. Product businesses are different from systems and installations businesses and technology fields are different from commodity fields. Each type of business has its own rules, its own challenges, and its own success factors.
In some areas of activity, standardization and process conformance are decisive for success. Producing a good result, such as high quality products, requires people to strictly follow the rules. In other businesses, like systems and installations, not everything can be standardized and cast in rules, and individual creativity is indispensable. Thus, the human factor has a

significantly higher relevance. Instead of expecting people to simply function like sprockets in a well lubricated machine, they have to be allowed and even encouraged to make certain decisions by themselves.

Therefore, each business requires a specific management approach. The assumption that a good manager in one business field will automatically be as good in another is simply wrong. Eventually, he or she could become a good manager, but not from the very beginning. Successful managers need to gain enough specific knowledge to understand the business, assess risks and opportunities, and make good decisions. Additionally, they need to get to know the people they are working with. Building personal relationships with their core team members, establishing mutual trust, and aligning the organization usually takes between six months to a year.

In many companies, the process of handing over the job from one manager to another does not receive enough attention. Sometimes, people are thrown into a new assignment without enough time for getting familiar with the new job. Additionally, it also happens quite often that managers who move into another position do not show much interest in spending too much effort on properly introducing their successor into the business. As a result, people often stumble completely unprepared into a new job and need too much time for getting up to speed.

Not understanding the new business well enough can lead to false expectations or erroneous assumptions. For example, managers coming from high-tech companies will usually not understand why a commodity business cannot yield the same level of profitability as their previous one. As another example, managers with a job history in businesses where reducing the number of working people through automation and process improvements is an important goal usually have difficulties understanding that in service—a people's business—people are indispensable. Not recognizing that especially in the service businesses well trained people are of highest value, they often perceive them as a liability.

Sometimes, hilarious situations arise when mangers starting in a new business meet their new people for the first time. On such an occasion, it may happen that completely different expectations are colliding and that both sides have the impression of dealing with extraterrestrials. Without knowing much about the new business, managers often confront their new organizations with unrealistic expectations. Even worse, they often swaggeringly refer to their old area of activity and make depreciative comments about what their new reports are presenting them. Often, discussions get stuck on the first presentation slide, and people do not even get the chance to explain their business. Such an ignorant and arrogant attitude can be observed quite often when managers start a new assignment. Instead of using the opportunity of a first encounter with their new people to make a good impression, new managers often succeed in shoveling a deep ditch between themselves and the rest of the organization right from the very beginning.

It is often the case that managers do not spent more than three to four years in one position before they are assigned to another. Depending on the size and complexity of the business, they may need up to a year to become familiar with the new field and another six months to hand over the business to their successor. Thus, the period during which they can act with full efficiency is rather short. Frequently changing managers also has another downside. Knowing that they will not be in this position long enough to suffer the consequences of their decisions and actions, mangers tend to accept unrealistic targets more easily. For the same reason, they would gear their efforts toward quick wins rather than toward the long-term sustainability of the business.

The effect of bad business plans on people is devastating because they lose confidence in their superiors and the company. They feel like being forced on a journey they do not want to make. Unachievable targets either demotivate people or make them do desperate things like engaging into high risk business transactions, violating rules and regulations, or even participating in fraudulent activities. The latter would apply for the recent diesel emissions scandal which is still shaking the automotive industry in Germany. Managers who are imposing unrealistic targets on their people usually do not have to fear any negative consequences in this regard. To the contrary, they are regarded as ambitious and entrepreneurial business leaders. The ones who have to suffer the consequences are the people responsible for fulfilling the plan. If they fail, they are held responsible, lose their incentives, are not promoted, and receive bad performance reviews. In this regard, the system is totally unfair.

Setting unachievable targets can turn into a serious business risk, like in the following example. As growing order intake numbers are generally regarded as an indication of a healthy business, a common mistake is frequently made by setting too ambitious targets for new orders. "We have to grow twice as much as the market," is a typical planning premise which often misguides to bad business plans. Setting these targets too high increases the likelihood of acquiring orders that will create problems during execution. Such 'bad orders' often lead to high costs of non-conformance, customer dissatisfaction, loss of reputation, and destruction of business values. They are a big burden for many companies.

In return, people try to protect themselves by 'sandbagging', which is defending targets below what they consider achievable. This is a widespread tactical method in this regard. Knowing that whatever they propose would be challenged by their managers, they go in as low as possible spending a lot of effort justifying why more would not be achievable. By emphasizing business risks and obscuring opportunities, people try to lower targets as much as possible to counterbalance their managers' exaggerated business expectations.

Suspecting most of their people of sandbagging, managers sometimes develop a real paranoia. It usually takes the form of demanding extreme transparency. Managers want their people to put all the cards on the table stripping them of any means to self-manage the financials of their business. They will usually insist on including all potential business opportunities in the plan but will be rather reluctant doing the same with the risks.

This is why, instead of being a joint effort to achieve the best for the company, business planning has become more of a boxing match between managers and their subordinates, in which the former are set for attack and the latter for defense. When the two parties, like opponents in the ring, concentrate more on setting the next blow, respectively on parrying it, business becomes a secondary issue. Often, arguments punch below the belt, and people take things personally.

Instead of representing a management instrument allowing everybody to contribute to the company's development, business planning often becomes a hated duty triggering nausea among all participants. The planning period usually leaves behind frustrated and demotivated people licking their wounds for some time before getting back to business.

In a business culture founded on mutual trust between managers and their people and based on fostering the entrepreneurial spirit throughout the entire organization, business planning must be a joint effort. To give their best efforts, people need to believe their targets are achievable. This does not mean that everybody needs to be in their comfort zone. To the contrary, most people need a challenge to achieve their best possible performance. If managers and their people have mutual trust, defining and achieving the targets should never be a problem.

Talking Chemistry

The Race Boat Analogy

Many businesses have excessive functional structures. Besides being an important cost factor, many staff functions add little value to the business and sometimes even impair the operational units in their work. In this regard, many companies resemble a boat with too many steersmen and too few rowers.

Normally, in a rowing boat the number of scullers should be greater than the number of coxes. One of the latter would be eventually needed, but in many cases the strokesman could take over his or her job. Common sense dictates that if somebody intended to make a boat as fast as possible, he or she would try out which combination was faster, the one with or the one without a cox. This means to assess the added value of this additional person for accomplishing the objective of winning the race. If coxes do not bring a decisive advantage, like observing the other competing teams and intelligently adapting the pace to save energy for the decisive sprint, they are only useless ballast. In race boats, like the ones battling in the Oxford–Cambridge race, everything is trimmed for performance. Because these races are not only decided by physical factors but also to a large extent by strategy and tactics, these boats have a steersman. While the scullers are big and powerful, he or she must be rather small and light-weighted. Even though it is common that rowers weigh 200 pound and more, nobody knowledgeable of this sport would come up with the idea of putting a 250 pound steersman onto the boat.

Therefore, it is quite surprising how many companies deviate from this simple logic—each additional pound the boat weighs must be compensated by the extra effort of the scullers—and carry 250 pound coxes in their organizations. In business, the operational units (the scullers) produce the business output, while staff units (the coxes) must ensure the appropriate pre-conditions enabling the former to develop their optimal perfor-mance, analogous to the roles in a race boat.

Are staff functions needed? By all means, yes! A complex busi-ness in a complex market cannot function without them. They are responsible for defining the strategies, observing competi-tion, analyzing the results, and providing the resources needed for the business.

Not different from a race boat, these functions must be lean and effective. Unfortunately, in many companies they are ex-actly the contrary.

An intrinsic problem of most larger organizations is that the ef-ficiency of staff functions can be assessed only by the staffers themselves. Who else other than the HR department of a com-pany would be able to determine how many people it needed. The same applies for strategy, controlling, marketing, and many other functional areas. If the heads and also the employ-ees of these departments were conscious that each additional pound they put on the scale would have to be compensated by the operational units, things would probably be easier to keep in good order. Because this is often not the case, staff depart-ments grow uncontrolled, often beyond what the business can afford. Why don't the people at the C-level of companies take corrective action? For top managers, staff functions have a similar role as court servants for kings in former times. When a king's entourage eventually became too expensive, he usually increased taxes instead of dismissing some of his court servants. Similarly, in many cases when functional costs explode, the managers responsible for the problem tend to pass the buck to the operational units by asking them to increase their profit contribution.

Not all businesses are alike. Therefore, the split of responsibilities and the relevance of staff functions may differ significantly. For example, the relevance of marketing in B2C businesses is usually much higher than in B2B ones. If customers cannot be reached at individual level, marketing campaigns make a lot of sense. In the smart phones business, knowing the specific preferences of the main target customer groups and directing product development, promotion, and advertising accordingly is mission-critical. This requires a high marketing effort. In B2B businesses, and especially if the majority of the market is made up by a limited number of large customers, such marketing effort would be a waste. Here, the relevant success factor is customer intimacy. This is something sales people, account managers, or the business heads themselves have to take care of; thus, marketing has a lower relevance.
It is imperative that businesses decide precisely in which area how much effort for non-productive activities has to be spent. In this regard, they must continuously assess the added value of such activities and terminate the ones with low business contribution.

Especially in larger companies, functional departments often become very big and develop their own dynamics. This makes streamlining them a difficult undertaking. They create new processes, new reports, and many other things of sometimes questionable value. Therefore, the load for the operational units increases, and the functional departments need even more people to process the additional information. One of the problems leading to those situations is that most people in functional departments are too far away from the business and even do not want to get too close to it. Many are completely lacking detailed subject matter expertise, which results in errors, friction, and slack.

For example, a clear directive is required with regard to where the business strategy is defined. These could be the business units themselves, defining and implementing their individual strategies, or it could be a central strategy office. In some companies, strategy definition is an ambiguous and inefficient mixture of both.

The role of strategy departments is to direct the future development of a business with regard to markets, business portfolio, and resources. Large companies usually have several strategy departments at different levels in charge of the above mentioned tasks. But often, most of the strategy work is carried out by the operational units themselves. Therefore, many of these strategy departments are not needed, at least not at the size they usually have. Their contribution is often limited to just providing templates, coordinating the efforts of the operational units, checking their input for formal consistency, and eventually compiling the individual strategies into one company strategy paper. Instead of steering the business development, many of these departments rather play the role of facilitators by acting as messengers between the CEO and the operational units. Because strategy people often do not have the required knowledge about the business, they are sometimes even hindering the process. Frequent results are, for example, errors regarding the correct understanding and communication of the CEO's directions, the provision of unsuitable templates, and the misinterpretation of business indicators. With regard to their rather limited role and little added value for the business, many strategy departments are over-staffed, and their salaries are too high.

HR departments also often generate too much functional costs for too little results. In addition to simply administering the company's human resources, they should also play the central role in the definition and implementation of the HR strategy. This comprises continuously assessing the health of the company's HR structure, identifying and recruiting the best people, and fostering the career development of employees. Instead, the operational units often take care of most of these tasks. The HR departments just support them on a generic level and offer little support when concrete action is required.

Controlling is another gray area where high functional costs are often unnecessarily produced. No doubt, regularly collecting, analyzing, and presenting financial business data is an important task. Nevertheless, with a well defined, precise, and efficient reporting process between the operational and the controlling units, this task could be completed with significantly less effort as it is often the case. It sometimes seems that the company's C-level needs controlling departments more to control the operational units rather than to control the business itself. The worse the business runs, the more efforts and monies are spent on controlling it. It is a widespread management error to assume that a business can be managed through controlling. When the business does not run well, all efforts need to be focused on improving the situation in the areas where value is generated. This is the place where the success of a business is determined. For example, if many large business endeavors exceed their budgets or have difficulties in providing the required level of quality, the root causes of these problems have to be immediately identified and addressed. This could be the case of poor program management, lack of resources, or low employee motivation. The specific problems have then to be mended at the operational level. Playing with numbers, preparing graphs and charts will not change anything. To the contrary, it just generates additional costs, leaving true problems unattended.

Inflated administrative structures and an unhealthy ratio between staff and operational people are an important cost factor and can result in the loss of the company's economic sustainability. The CEO's duty, among others, is to define the way the organization has to function and to assign clear responsibilities to the different departments. In this regard, it is especially important to avoid redundancies. Redundancy is a typical problem of companies with excessive administrative structures. If something is covered by the operational units, it is not necessary and most times even counter-productive having somebody in a functional department doing the same thing. Even though it seems obvious, in many companies such overlap can still be observed. Usually, these problems do not get addressed directly. This could be accomplished by systematically assessing the added value of all staff functions and by eliminating the ones with questionable value contribution. Instead, just rather generic reduction programs for administration costs are initiated, "Reduce admin costs by 15%!", with the frequent result that those costs are just pushed into operations without really improving the situation. It is often the case that especially in a crisis scenario when the company is not performing well, administration costs are even driven up by introducing new structures and functions and by engaging external consultants to address the bad situation.

It is quite astonishing sometimes seeing people in the organization, with nobody exactly knowing what they do. They have always been around, and nobody questions their presence. In deed, large and complex organizations are a good hiding place for people who do not necessarily add value to the business. They are either connected to important persons in the company or are able to smartly protect their position. It is a simple matter of organizational hygiene to reassign them to a useful job or to remove them from the organization.

Typical job titles for people of sometimes questionable value for the business are 'Director of something'. Directors usually have no direct accountability, and the success of their work is rather difficult to measure. Determining which of these functions a company needs should be solely based on (demonstrated) added value. The approach 'Put them in, and only if the boat gets faster, keep them' should rule any decision in this regard. Sometimes, the value of support functions is difficult to assess. For example, in a large international business, a particular region may have performed extremely well. Should these results be attributed to the valuable guidance provided by the central strategy and business development departments, or should they rather be credited to the local operational units for doing a good job? Most times, the former will take credit of the success. "The business volume in my region of responsibility grew by x% over the last three years," people in the headquarters sometimes blatantly say expecting that everybody recognizes their outstanding contribution. A closer look often tells a different story revealing that the dedicated work of the regional people was the true success factor. Nevertheless, in large businesses with international presence, business development is an important task. The typical role of business development people is to open new business opportunities, to develop new markets, and to support the international sites. They can have a significant contribution in setting up businesses, negotiating important contracts, mobilizing projects, and in improving business performance. To be successful, they need excellent subject matter expertise, strong entrepreneurial spirit, and good social and intercultural competence. They also need to have a decisive edge over the people in the regional offices. Many business developers do not meet these requirements. This function is often abused as a parking position for people who cannot be used somewhere else. Instead of actively engaging in the business, many business developers act more as spectators. Their activities are limited to visiting business sites, gathering information, collecting data for reporting purposes, and communicating instructions and business targets from the head office. Many of them learn about the business from the people they are supposed to support. They assume limited responsibility for what is happening in their business area. If things go well, they will take a step up. If things go wrong, they prefer staying in the shadow blaming the failure on the operational sites. In many cases, the business value generated by these functions does not justify the high costs associated with them.

Functional organizations are especially prone to redundancy, inefficiency and high coordination effort. If sales, operations, supply chain, and R&D are set up as functional departments, none of them has an end to end business responsibility. The only one responsible for the overall result is the company's CEO. In most cases, he or she is overwhelmed by the complexity and number of tasks. Each department is contributing with its own share without a real concern about how the different parts fit together. When the final solution is aggregated, everybody is surprised to find out that what was delivered is not what was planned or what the customer has ordered.

Operational people do not have much of an understanding for the effort and money which is sometimes wasted in functional departments. They see them continuously growing while having difficulties in getting the resources approved they need to do their job. They constantly get confronted with challenges to increase the operational profit, sometimes beyond the intrinsic capabilities of the business. In the long run, such a situation wears people out, kills their motivation, and makes them lose the belief into the business and into their managers.

Unattended, a situation where businesses are struggling with constantly growing functional costs and progressively degrading operational performance can easily end up in a death spiral.

Talking Chemistry

The Death Spiral

Death spirals, also called graveyard spirals, are known from airplanes and are the nightmare of every pilot. Similarly to aviation, death spirals can occur in business as well. They do not happen accidentally. Most of them are a direct consequence of management failures due to incapability, ignorance, overestimation, or misguided pride.

When an airplane gets trapped in a death spiral, it is usually the result of the pilots being misled by their senses in bad weather conditions and of their inability to correctly process the information provided by the flight instruments. Sometimes, a death spiral can also be caused by the failure of an important system or a component of the airplane. This dangerous dive usually ends when the plane hits the ground. Generally, in aviation death spirals are the result of a combination of physical and psychological factors.

A company can also enter into a death spiral when managers fail to maintain its competitiveness and to recognize changes in the business environment. As in this case physical aspects usually have no relevance, the managers who allow their business getting in such a dangerous situation have to take the blame alone. There are many triggers which can initiate a death spiral. These could be external reasons such as a decrease in market demand or a changing competitive environment. But there are also many internal root causes which can lead to a business downturn: a wrong portfolio, an aging organization, unrealistic business targets, an inappropriate organizational set-up, operational inefficiency, or low personnel motivation. Even though usually just one of these aspects initiates the spiral, if it remains unaddressed, other aspects will soon be adding to it, accelerating the fall. Sooner or later, the situation escalates to the point where managers completely lose control and do not know which strings to pull first.

Even though the result is mostly the same, the crash of the airplane respectively of the business, not all death spirals are of the same nature. For example, the downturn of the traditional watch making industry occurring after the invention of quartz watches was inevitable. Suddenly, everyone wanted quartz watches because they were fashionable, cheap, and especially because they were more precise. In a very short period of time, mechanical watch making lost its business base. As a result, many brands came close to bankruptcy or disappeared completely. Was such a turn in market demand foreseeable? Possibly yes. Was the dramatic business situation avoidable? Probably not. Even though Switzerland was leading the development of quartz watch mechanisms and more domestic manufactures could have recognized its extraordinary relevance, switching to this totally new technology in such a short period of time would have been a very difficult undertaking. All traditional brands went into a death spiral fighting with the dramatic reduction in market demand for their products. Some of them crashed; others managed to survive a hard landing and were able to come back when the market conditions changed again and wearing mechanical watches became a sign of exclusivity and a factor of distinction. These days, traditional car manufacturers are facing a similar situation, although the speed of change is slower. Those companies who will hit the curve apex best by capitalizing maximally on the profits conventional cars still yield and by investing at the right time into new technologies to enter the age of electric mobility with full speed will be successful. All other companies will end up as niche players or will completely vanish.

Different from the above examples, other death spirals happen under intact market conditions and are the result of bad management, which makes them especially deplorable.
Such a death spiral can be initiated by setting unrealistic business targets. Too ambitious growth plans bear many risks, for example, when a company's execution capabilities cannot keep pace with the volume of new orders. When too many orders need to be executed simultaneously and personnel resources are scarce, execution quality usually suffers. Technical errors and delays drive costs up and eventually also trigger penalties and other contractual fines. A couple of those bad orders can easily deteriorate the profitability of the entire business. People are being chased from one site to another to close gaps and are driven to exhaustion. As a result, they lose their motivation, and errors become even more frequent. Finally, bad quality increasingly dissatisfies customers. Suddenly, nothing seems to fit any longer. Common for most death spirals is that managers refuse to recognize the real causes and therefore initiate the wrong measures. Regardless of the root cause of the problem, most managers start with cutting costs by all means. Bureaucratic hurdles such as special approval for all kinds of expenditures are set up, and hiring stops for urgently needed operational personnel are imposed without reflection. Such measures possibly slow down the descent without really stopping it. Often, they even accelerate the fall.

Talking Chemistry

Paradoxically, in troubled companies the administrative over-heads seem to even grow. Instead of focusing on solving the real problems, managers often spend even more efforts and resources on controlling them, which only worsens the overall situation.

The fundamental question that needs to be answered before defining any improvement strategy is whether the company still possesses the intrinsic capabilities of a recovery. In this regard, the two most important elements are a sufficient num-ber of capable and still motivated managers and a still com-mitted workforce. Under these premises, a recovery could be possible, and the CEO must take the role of the turnaround manager. Introducing another person to this role only means disclaiming the CEO's mandate to run the business.

No matter how it starts, when a company is caught in a death spiral, nothing seems to work any longer. Poor execution causes customer dissatisfaction. Customers do not trust the company any longer and stop placing new orders. With the sales pipeline progressively drying out, management becomes increasingly reluctant to hire new people. Good people leave the company, and mediocrity prevails. This is also the moment when competitors start aggressively raiding the best people, and it is especially painful seeing the business champions change sides and take the company's knowledge with them. Usually, the managers fail to recognize the true dimension of the problem. Sometimes, because they do not receive accurate information from the levels below. Sometimes, because they prefer to ignore what they do not want to hear. Naturally, un-der these circumstances, they send totally wrong signals to their organization, aggravating the situation even more.

External consultants are often hired to assess the situation and to propose solutions. Being usually rather expensive, they represent an additional significant cost burden for the company. Most consultants start by conducting extensive interviews with the company's managers, thus keeping them from doing their job. In many cases, consultants do not possess sufficient subject matter expertise of the business they are supposed to assess and thus are trying to solve the problem with a generic approach. Therefore, they usually provide generic results. When they finally present their findings, most people are surprised to hear what they already knew.

Eventually, the head of the company hires new managers to replace those who are made responsible for the poor business condition. In singular cases, this could be a solution. But usually, it does not work either for the following two reasons. The new managers are confronted with unfavorable preconditions like missing or inappropriate process descriptions, unclear responsibilities, and ambiguous interface specifications. Overwhelmed by the complexity of the challenge and tired of fighting wind mills, many of them give up after a couple of months. Additionally, a new manager needs about half a year to become familiar with a complex business. In a death spiral, time is of the essence. There is no grace period, and fast action is required.

For all of these reasons, a recovery from such a situation is so difficult.

In the majority of cases, the person at the top of a company, its CEO, bears the responsibility for such a business downturn. Not different from the captain of the airplane, it is the CEO's job to constantly assess the business situation and adapt the

cruise accordingly. Like the pilot who must be able to antici-
pate a dangerous storm, he or she must foresee changes in
the business environment, like market demand and competition. In their decision making, managers must use the results
of business analytics as well as other supporting information
provided by their reports. Rather than relying blindly on such
information, they must assess it with their own business sense.

As most death spirals end in a crash, obviously, the main objective must be avoiding them. CEOs must start each working
day by asking themselves "Are we still on track?" Regular
management meetings concentrate mainly on current operational issues and generally do not address the general business
situation well enough. CEOs should encourage their reports to
regularly reflect on the above question and openly communicate their respective opinion. This way, the managers would
receive valuable information about how the company is really
doing and where potential dangers could be hidden. Unfortunately, many managers do not appreciate open opinions, especially if they do not agree with their own ideas.

There are many early indicators which could indicate a business downturn that could eventually end in a death spiral.
An interesting approach to avoid such an undesirable situation
would be to develop a company health map covering all critical
business aspects including: (1) Markets, Customers, and Demand; (2) Business Portfolio and Innovation; (3) Competitors;
(4) Partners and Suppliers; (5) Sales; (6) Operations; (7) Human Resources and Organizational Hygiene; and (8) Financials. This map structure could be individually adapted according to the special needs of any particular business. A scor-
ing system ranging from 1 (on track) through 3 (requires
immediate action) to 5 (extremely critical) and a specific set of

evaluation criteria shall be used to assess the health of each of the above areas. By regularly updating this health map during management meetings, for instance on a half-yearly basis, the question "Are we still on track?" could be answered in a more objective manner. "Have we identified all relevant changes in the market and have we adapted our strategy and our portfolio accordingly?" "Have we elaborated individual development plans for all our strategic customers and are we well positioned from a sales perspective?" The advantage of such an approach is that it formally forces managers to regularly ascertain the situation of their business and to take corrective action if required. Most managers address an issue only when it becomes critical, instead of tackling it when first signs of unhealthiness become visible. For example, everybody seems surprised when a company's personnel structure gets overaged or when indispensable specialists go into retirement with nobody to replace them. A health map would force the CEO and his or her head of HR to start addressing the problem when there is still time. As part of this process, they would have to also answer the question "Is there a replacement for every key position in the company identified and nominated *well in advance* before this person leaves for retirement?" If, for example, *well in advance* were longer than two years, the situation would be on track. If it were only one year, this would require immediate action. And if it were even less than that, the situation would be extremely critical and needs to be urgently addressed.

Many bad surprises, such as companies suddenly getting caught in a downward swirl, could have been avoided if the respective advisory boards had asked their CEOs to update and present such a health map on a regular basis.

Escaping from a death spiral is difficult because apparently there is no firm grip on the problem. Everything is moving, and nothing seems to be stable. It is impossible to address all points at the same time. Therefore, it is essential to narrow down all efforts on the root cause and to not spend too much time on those elements which would automatically fix themselves once the root cause gets solved. For example, if as a result of poor execution customers are dissatisfied, employees get demotivated, and the general business situation is deteriorating, it does not make much sense to push on sales. Every new order would aggravate the situation even more. In such a case, research and development also becomes a secondary aspect. Thus, additional engineering resources could be redirected to assist operations by helping to sort out the problems at operational level. Good co-operation of the entire management team is mission-critical in such a situation. Finger-pointing and cross-blaming do not help. It is the CEO's role to align everybody in a concerted effort toward the common goal of escaping the death spiral. Another important aspect is to make sure that people do not get the impression of being left alone with their problems. CEOs and COOs must regularly visit the operational sites and acknowledge their support. They also must regularly see customers and demonstrate their personal commitment. Once the operational aspects get back on track, the tension on the customer side will automatically ease up, and employee motivation will gradually be restored.

When a company eventually escapes a death spiral, the CEO and the other top managers may regard it as a proof of their management skills, celebrating themselves as business heroes. This can easily become the starting point for the next death spiral. They may forget that they were responsible for it in the first place and that by allowing the situation to deteriorate to such an extent, they have destroyed a lot of company good will. Something else that is usually forgotten in such a situation is the fact that restoring the company's health was primarily the result of the hard work and sacrifices of the workforce.

Talking Chemistry

The Ego Trap

"I am the greatest!" This is something not only Mohammad Ali once thought about himself. Many business managers also think of themselves as being extraordinary and gifted with out-standing talents. Trapped inside their own 'Me' (ego), they put themselves above everything. As a result of a distorted com-prehension of the reality around them, their self-image is often far beyond their true capabilities and achievements.

Do business managers need a big ego to be successful? Some-times, a big ego helps one to become a manager in the first place. It is not mandatory though. The sound belief in the own capabilities coupled with perseverance are more solid qualities for a future good manager and better reasons for professional success. Even though it may take a little bit longer to build, a manager career based on true values leads to higher profes-sional recognition and personal satisfaction. Determining what makes a manager successful requires defining first what suc-cess means in this regard. Many managers define success by climbing as high as possible in the company hierarchy in the shortest period of time. For them, the value they generate for the business and the legacy they leave behind in their different positions are of secondary importance. Everything is about themselves. Unfortunately, today's business culture fosters such people. Most companies send potential young talents to assessment centers to verify their suitability for a future man-agement career. In such workshops, usually lasting a couple of days, auditors create an artificial environment confronting candidates with different business-like tasks and situations. Their behavior and reactions are deemed a reliable indication of their managerial talents. Based on the concept 'We can assess only what we can see,' assessment centers are in favor of those candidates who manage to establish the highest visibility and exposure during this short period of time. Fundamental qualities such as a good character, endurance, honesty, and loyalty cannot be made visible during these workshops. Another reason why assessment centers do not necessarily select the best candidates is the fact that most participants are playing a role, acting accordingly to what they think the auditors want to see. There are courses offered by various institutions and consultants specially geared at preparing people for such assessments. Those candidates winning the race to the presentation board will be the most successful. In real business life, good managers rather let their people present the results of their work and refrain from standing in the limelight.

True managers define success by the business value generated together with their people. They do not perceive their position as something they are owed because of their extraordinary capabilities. They see it as a privilege and consider themselves servants of their business. For them, it is very important what their employees really think about them. Instead of suffocating everybody with their presence, they are creating a working environment centered around the business and not around themselves where everybody can capitalize best on his or her individual capabilities and creativity. They emanate sovereignty, self-confidence, authenticity, and trustworthy in a natural way sometimes difficult to explain. It is just there.

An exaggerated ego is totally incompatible with this a kind of managers. It would impair them recognizing the successes of their employees, as a team and as individuals. It would make them perceive the presence of strong and talented people in their organization as a threat rather than a gift.

What people call a 'big ego' psychology defines as egotism.

Egotism is the drive to maintain and enhance favorable views of oneself, and generally features an inflated opinion of one's personal features and importance. It often includes intellectual, physical, social and other overestimations.[1]
The egotist has an overwhelming sense of the centrality of the 'Me', that is to say of their personal qualities.[2] Egotism means placing oneself at the center of one's world with no concern for others, including those 'loved' or considered as 'close', in any other terms except those subjectively set by the egotist.[3]

It seems appropriate calling managers fitting into the above described character pattern **ego managers**.

Moderate egotism is not unusual and occasionally it can be useful, in private life and in professional life as well.

Egotism may help people escaping the paralyzing effects of self-doubt, motivate them to pursue difficult and imposing goals, and reduce the shame of personal failure.[4]

---

[1] Robin M Kowalski ed., Aversive Interpersonal Behaviors (1977)

[2] William Walker Atkinson, The New Psychology (2010)

[3] Burgess-Jackson,, K (2013). "Taking Egoism Seriously". Ethical theory and moral practice,.

[4] Anthony G. Greenwald (1980)

Excessive egotism, though, is an ugly aversive behavior. Obviously, such chemistry is poison for any environment, including business. It negates the essence of an organization and reduces it to the role of the ego manager's entourage. Those subordinates engaging into playing this role will be favored; those still insisting on having an own opinion and initiative will be treated with suspicion. Over time, the ego manager will gather around him or her a group of servile people entirely dedicated to supporting his or her role and strongly concerned to protect their own position. They will engage into an internal race for becoming the manager's #1 favorite. Those who the ego manager considers 'loyal' will benefit from various favors, such as a better income, larger freedom for action in less important matters, and tolerance regarding own failures. This odd setup resembling to a medieval king's court paralyzes organizational development and inhibits good people in pursuing their professional goals. Eventually, ego managers will accept the presence of people with exceptional business talents in their organization. This happens especially in the case of subject matter experts capable of solving difficult problems. Rather than perceiving them as valuable contributors to the business, the ego manager regards them more as personal trophies which he or she can send into the battle whenever the going gets tough. "I'm sending in _my_ best man," is more the self-confirmation of one's own managerial talents and less an appreciation for the best man's capabilities.

Arrogance and hubris are two toxic facets that usually come together in most ego managers. Considering themselves infallible, they often take decisions arbitrarily without consulting their people. "You're free to have your own opinion as long as you keep it to yourself, and don't ever attempt to question my own decisions," denotes their distorted understanding of the organization's role. Even though disrespectful and offending, most people accept this attitude for the sake of their own comfort. Those who do not will be pushed to the sideline or will be forced to leave the organization.

Considering themselves superior to the people surrounding them, ego managers usually react negatively to criticism. They often take criticism personally and consider the people criticizing them enemies. Occasionally, they take moderate negative comments as a pleasantry. It flatters them. "I always hated being perfect, what a privilege it is to also have a weakness." Therefore, ego managers do not see a reason for working on their profile and stay trapped inside their habits.

People driven by their own ego generally harmonize well with other people when the relationship is unequivocal. They get along well with their subordinates, as long as they are in the good category and accept their assigned roles. They usually also get well along with their bosses, especially if an attempt of taking over their position has to be considered 'A Bridge Too Far'. Interaction at eye level with peers usually ends in a disaster. Egotists simply cannot accept other people at the same level. Instead of working together toward a common goal, they will spend most of their energy to subdue others and to win the favor of their bosses. Such internal fights can be often observed when organizational competencies and business mandates are distributed.

Most ego managers consider themselves the #1 success factor in the organization. This can be true for small privately owned companies where one person is the owner, the boss, and also the business itself and where all others are simply helpers. It is also true for people with exceptional talents who have forged trendsetting businesses and have changed entire activity sectors and sometimes even the entire world with their visions and ideas. Without them, these companies would not exist. For most larger companies, success is the result of the collective effort of all employees over a longer period of time. Certainly, management decisions have a decisive role, but failure and especially success are much harder to individualize. Like a big supertanker, large companies have massive inertia which makes them less sensitive to individual business decisions and will keep them on course even in stormy whether. Therefore, everybody claiming business success for him or herself in such companies shall be treated with suspicion.

Certainly, people at the top of large organizations must emanate a certain aura. Managers must give their people everything they need to have the feeling of following the right person. It is this special mixture of closeness to people and distinction at the same time which makes great leaders so unique, reserving them a prominent place in the company's legacy.
Egotistical persons will never develop a positive aura and will never generate a genuine pull effect on their employees. If they leave, the only things left behind in the organization are relief and the feeling of wasted time and lost opportunities.

For all of these reasons, ego managers represent a significant business risk for their companies. Too often, such persons have brought initially prosperous businesses into trouble or even destroyed them. Weirdly enough, they repeatedly succeed to deceive the people surrounding them and to climb the career ladder up to the top level of companies. Unmasking ego managers and not allowing them to play their ugly games should be strongly anchored in the business culture of any company.

Managers have a decisive influence on the careers of people. Good managers are capable of unleashing the potential of their employees and of helping them become good managers them-selves. They will do their best to balance the requirements of the business with the requirements of their people. Bad man-agers suffocate their people and hinder them from becoming what they could be.

Therefore, whenever possible, people should carefully choose their managers. For those looking for a ticket to a comfortable business life with moderate effort, an ego manager could be the right choice. Those preferring an environment in which they are encouraged to capitalize best on their talents and in which they can fulfill their professional aspirations must choose a manager with collaborative management style and for which business comes first.

Talking Chemistry

The Value Chimera

Corporate Values are very en vogue today. Company websites and annual reports provide extensive information about the values companies share. With almost no exception, Corporate Responsibility is the first item on a company's value list. Responsibility toward society, employees, shareholders, environment, and so on. Responsibility toward everybody and everything. This flood of generic company values dilutes the focus on genuine core values which employees can embrace and use as a guideline for their professional acts and attitudes. Therefore, forging a positive business culture based on true values often remains a chimera—just an illusion.

The recent scandals observed in the banking community and various industrial sectors, such as in the car industry, require a critical review of the value campaigns of most companies. The destruction of such an incredible amount of company value and reputation in such a short period of time is a serious treason against all company stakeholders. If all the values these companies proclaim and all the responsibility statements they make had a true meaning, such bad developments would not have been possible. Can these incidents be regarded as isolated occurrences? There are good reasons that they are not.

With the development of the Internet and the increased public exposure, a real competition between companies about the hippest corporate values has started. Corporate responsibility has become a formal structural and organizational element of companies, with specially dedicated people and departments watching over it. Since decades, every new employee receives elaborate information about the company values he or she is expected to share. With each promotion or transfer to another department or area of activity, the appeal for supporting the company's values is renewed. Therefore, it can be assumed that all employees have sufficient information about the company values so they can understand and embrace them.

Well, do they?

Let us assume for a moment they do. Let us assume that the majority of the employees genuinely share these values and feel compelled to support them. In this case, incidents like the recent car manufactures scandals related to the violation of emission standards are not explicable. One of the leading car companies involved in this affair pinpoints environmental, product, and social responsibility as well as responsibility toward its workforce as the leading elements of its corporate identity. But cars substantially exceeding advertised emission values and possibly infringing on binding standards do not comply with any of these values mentioned above. If negligence had been the root cause, it would have been only half as bad. Improved processes, additional checkpoints, and better controls would then have been adequate solutions for the problem. Unfortunately, negligence cannot serve as an excuse in this case. Willful misconduct, carefully planned and disguised, was the cause. Debating about right or wrong in this particular case would be redundant effort. There are enough law firms, governmental entities, and the press already doing it. Instead, the following focuses on the sustainability of currently practiced corporate value campaigns.

If conscious about their environmental, social, and product responsibility, why would motor engineers dedicate their creativity to developing a product that betrays all corporate values? It harms the environment because of excessive emissions, cheats society as a result of illegitimately avoided emission taxes, rips off shareholders in terms of lost company value, and endangers the job security of its workforce. It also betrays the environmental conscience of customers and jeopardizes their mobility because of possible car bans from urban centers.

Such incidents of misconduct will continue to happen because the behavior of employees is determined predominantly by other factors than the corporate values proclaimed by most companies. This general phenomenon can be observed across all economic areas. Selling high risk financial products to elderly people as a back up for their retirement or granting questionable loans to persons not qualified to receive them are just a couple of other examples from the banking community for situations when employees completely ignore corporate values. When confronted with the prospect of immense bonuses or with the threat of losing the job, corporate values become a secondary issue, something remote and obscure. They are somewhere there, but they do not govern individual acts and behaviors. Therefore, most current value campaigns are a waste of time, money, and resources. They do not change the behavior of employees, and they do not generate any business benefit either. Some usually smaller and very often family owned companies are an exception. Here, values are genuine part of the company's legacy and have been carefully preserved throughout the years in the hearts and souls of their owners and employees. In most larger companies, the values are designed by special professionals in the corporate departments. These corporate people, most of them

with similar educational backgrounds, social views, and professional predilections, usually build a company's value schema
out of a tool kit. Therefore, most value statements are alike,
centered on responsibility and correctness toward everybody
and everything. They sound academic and complicated and do
not provide any differentiation or real decision support for employees, customers, or shareholders.

A successful value campaign was conducted in a large German
corporation in the aftermath of a big corruption scandal. Inevitably, this campaign also included many value related arguments such as responsibility, honesty, and integrity, which, by
the way, were already introduced long before. But what really
changed people's behavior was the simple message "In any
case of fraud or serious misconduct, the company will immediately terminate you," Bam! "You will be personally confronted
with the law, and we will no longer support you," Bam! "Your
liberty and your personal wealth will be in jeopardy." Bam! It
went like a shock wave throughout the company and scared
everybody to death. Extensive new controls and regulations
aimed at prevention and early detection of misconduct were
established. The conduct guidelines were updated and handed
out to all employees. But the real difference was made by the
constant repetition of the same message "You mess up, you'll
be on your own" until it became hardwired in people's minds.
In a couple of years the company made it up to the top of all
international corporate integrity rankings.
The conclusion to be drawn from this example is obvious, even
though disappointing. Many employees do not really care
about abstract corporate values like the ones promoted in
most value campaigns. They perceive them as academic, artificial and as a must-have gimmick. In the absence of direct

personal consequences, most people will choose the easiest way directed to their personal advantage.

How can a sustainable corporate culture where corporate values influence people's professional behavior still be established? A first step would be recognizing that corporate culture is determined by the individual beliefs, behaviors, and goals of all company employees rather than by a formal value scheme. Individual behavior is influenced by the following factors in the order of relevance: (1) fear of repercussions, for example as a consequence of professional misconduct; (2) stimulus from rewards like promotion, salary increase and bonuses; (3) personal motivation triggered by various aspects including educational background, moral views, and especially the bonding with the company. These three factors apply for the vast majority of people, even though for some individuals the order could be different.

Therefore, forging a positive corporate culture should include all factors mentioned above. Fostering the personal motivation of employees and implementing a working climate centered around personal responsibility are the two most important elements in this regard.

Different people are motivated by different things. While some are motivated by visions and missions, most employees are rather motivated by more traditional values like a fair and respectful treatment including fair pay, the company's tradition, and the making of good products that satisfy customers.

Employees who are genuinely willing to engage in maintaining and developing the company's legacy are especially valuable. Those people would not allow getting cajoled into bad games such as cheating or corruption. Unfortunately, current management styles do not really foster such employees because they increasingly ignore traditions and do not honor any personal goodwill employees may have accrued over the years. Being just as good as one's last mistake is not really motivating.

The value of traditions for the business culture of a company is enormous. Traditions link people together and make them feel part of a greater success story. Though, they are often neglected—mostly because many companies shy away from the effort and the costs associated with keeping traditions alive. As a young engineer, I was part of the central service group for industrial computers and automation systems of a large company. We were forming the third (and last) service escalation level for this type of equipment. If one of us had failed in solving a problem, the consequences for our customers and also for our company would have been severe. We were traveling most of the time from one project site to another and did not see our colleagues for months. But once a year, all of us came together for our 'Service Day' which was celebrated shortly before Christmas at the company headquarters. Everybody (except those who were urgently needed on site) was expected to participate, and travel costs were no issue. During the day we presented our different projects and shared our experiences, and in the evening everybody came together for the gala dinner. In the abundantly decorated huge company canteen, we enjoyed excellent food and select wines served by uniformed waiters. The company asked for much, but we could see that in return the company cared for us. This was our evening and missing this day was no option. We felt like the 'Delta Force' of the company, ready to embrace any challenge. Even today, these 'Service Days' are still in my memory and give me the feeling of having been part of something special that fills me with pride.

In order to develop personal motivation geared at supporting the success of the business, people need to be able to believe in their company and in their managers. Because this kind of motivation resides in their hearts and souls, it trumps all other stimuli. It is also harder to establish and to maintain.

Ensuring that every employee embraces personal responsibility is evenly important and difficult. The biggest obstacle in this regard is the socialization of responsibility. This bad habit can be observed in most companies, especially in the larger ones. Meetings and workshops are perfect instruments to dilute personal accountability. For most people, a problem loses its criticality once it can be shared with others. Shortly after it was communicated to their managers and superiors are in the loop, an issue suddenly becomes everybody's problem. This phenomenon can be observed throughout all company levels all the way up to the top. Another very popular manager trick aimed at reducing the personal accountability is to engage external consultants. But if responsibility is not individualized, it is worthless. Collective responsibility is a very vague term. What is corporate responsibility after all? Whose heads will roll if the company fails? Like in recent car manufactures and banking scandals, the main consequence for the involved companies were hefty fines. These fines went into the company ledger, and in the end everybody was more or less well off; except the shareholders who were hit by a massive decrease of their shares value. Only in very few cases, in which managers have not only betrayed company values but also grossly conflicted with the law, pursuance has triggered more painful individual consequences. Mismanagement is largely tolerated, and it often takes years until a manager eventually gets fired. If managers were required to make a personal (monetary) security deposit for the soundness of their business decisions and for the compliance of their actions, the situation would immediately change dramatically.

Often, the refusal of superiors to accept a "NO" from their subordinates is the starting point for bad business practices. "I won't take 'NO' for an answer!" is what people often hear from their bosses. They are left alone with a serious problem, like a business target they do not know how to achieve or a technical challenge for which they do not have a solution. In such situations, people sometimes do foolish things. In the aftermath of a big scandal, most managers try to wash their hands of any responsibility by pretending "We didn't know!" Apart from the fact that it is their job to know, hiding behind their subordinates just to save their own neck is simply repugnant.

Making a wrong business decision may cost one's job; breaking the law may cost people their freedom. When complex business, technical, legal, and social requirements need to be taken into consideration and balanced against each other, decision making is like walking a fine line. Therefore, in many tight business situations good legal support is of the essence. Exhausting the boundaries of what is permitted might sometimes be questionable from another point of view but still required from a business perspective. Aiming to protect the company's reputation and to preserve its legacy and tradition often helps in finding the right balance in this regard.

Politicians also have to take the blame. Responsibility toward society or environment is not the first obligation of companies. This statement may be provocative. Nevertheless, it is still valid. Companies are business assets supposed to yield a profit and produce something customers want to buy. In achieving these goals, they are primarily required to act inside the boundaries set by the law. Where corrupt governments, incompetent politicians, and poor legal enforcement fail in setting these boundaries and in imposing painful sanctions upon illegal activities, it would be foolish to expect companies to voluntarily set their own limits.

In the German diesel scandal, managers abused poor homologation procedures defined by government-controlled technical entities. The same is true for the bad things that happened in the banking community. Many financial products of questionable customer value receive the approval from the respective financial authorities.

No wonder why companies capitalize on such opportunities. Creatively dealing with technical or financial regulations inside the allowed is often a question of survival in the marketplace, also because nobody can assume that the competition is not acting the same way. It is quite surprising that in Germany collusion is generally not considered a criminal offense and the only thing companies have to fear are fines. In almost all cases, these fines were substantially lower than the extra profits companies made by breaking antitrust laws. The damage incurred by customers, like from price-fixing, is of no real concern for anybody.

Some readers may ask how ESG (Environmental Social Governance) fits into this picture. ESG does not define and does not produce corporate values. It defines the self-imposed rules and boundaries according to and in between which the company must act with regard to environmental and social aspects.

As ESG increasingly gets into the focus of investors, it should be anchored in the company's strategy.

To improve their corporate culture, many companies need to reconsider their current approaches. In this regard, the following factors would have a positive influence:

- A transparent and collaborative management style governed by respect and fairness
- Concentration on essential corporate values such as customer value, long-term business sustainability, and the company's tradition and legacy
- Implementation of a personal responsibility system, especially at management level
- A zero tolerance policy related to fraudulent activities and misconduct

Businesses should focus on those values which have a real meaning for their stakeholders—customers, shareholders, and employees. Customers should be able to trust in receiving an honest and useful product, shareholders to rely on the diligent treatment of their investment, and employees to believe in finding their professional home rewarding them fairly for their efforts and allowing them to capitalize on their capabilities.

Everything else is useless ballast.

The Motivation Matrix

Motivation is what drives every endeavor. People do or refrain from doing things out of their personal motivation. Positive motivation unleashes the total potential of people and is an important success factor for companies. Therefore, it is quite surprising that most managers do not think about what motivates their people. Therefore, they often fail in developing the appropriate personnel strategies.

Even though one could think that in business any source of motivation is desirable, some kinds of motivation have to be questioned. Not all of them guarantee long-term business success. Some kinds of motivation have only short-term relevance, others can easily turn into the opposite. Thus, managers should dedicate some of their efforts to understanding what drives their people. The managers' knowledge of the individual motivation of their employees is especially relevant with regard to the members of their core team and also with regard to the high-performers and the incumbents of key functions in their organization. The higher employees rank in the company, the more important it is for their superiors to know what motivates them.

In business, the following four sources of motivation are the most relevant:

Fear is one of our basic emotions and the strongest source of motivation for most people. Though formerly very useful for ensuring survival out in the wild, in today's business, fear is a bad source of motivation. Unfortunately, it can be encountered quite often. Many people are driven in their jobs by the fear of professional failure, the fear of their superiors, or very often by the fear of losing their jobs. This kind of motivation can be observed especially during company restructurings and rationalizations when people significantly increase their work efforts because of their fear of being laid off. The worst aspect about fear is that it inhibits the creativity of people. Fear kills the entrepreneurial spirit and lets everybody follow the known and safe path. In critical situations, fear can push people short-term going the extra mile, but it cannot serve as a sustainable source of motivation.

Rewards are the most common source of positive motivation, also in business. Most people are motivated by receiving rewards. They are even more motivated in the anticipation of them.

Money is the most common stimulus. If the financial situation of the company allows for it, rewarding excellent work with additional money is a good solution, but its effect is only temporary. Even though for some people the fair pay for their work is already a reward strong enough to keep them motivated, most people expect an income increase or a promotion to keep up their commitment. Many fail to understand that delivering a good result is part of their job. Thus, as their effort is already compensated by their pay, it would not be justified expecting more without further increasing the contribution to the company. As a stimulus, money is subject to high depreciation. After a short period of time, most people would take a salary increase for granted and wait for the next one. Some people have little understanding that monetary rewards cannot be granted if the business situation of the company is bad. Such an attitude would be eventually acceptable in the lower ranks. In the case of managers, it puts a big question mark behind their professional integrity.

Promoting people just to keep up their motivation is not a good tactic either. Promotions are primarily an instrument of organizational hygiene and should not be abused as a stimulus. They should be the result of a sustained and long-term effort in combination with excellent results. People should be promoted into higher positions only on the basis of their demonstrated higher capabilities and the benefit they have generated for the business. Promotion opportunities attract job hoppers who are in constant search for chances to climb the career ladder by changing jobs. They tend to stay in a job just as long as required to gather enough arguments for the next promotion but never long enough for having to deal with the long-term consequences of their business decisions. The added value of such people is questionable.

In conclusion, because a company cannot constantly increase salaries or promote people, rewards are not a good instrument to ensure long-term motivation. To the contrary, people getting used to money or promotion related stimuli will often soon lose their motivation in the absence of these benefits. If money or promotions are a person's sole source of motivation, building personnel alternatives in time is imperative.

As a special kind of reward, fame can be a very strong motivator. People stimulated by fame will keep up their motivation as long as they are allowed to be heroes. Thirst for fame and for being praised can push people to outstanding achievements, but, on the other hand, it can also mislead them to take hazardous business decisions. They are hard workers and spend a lot of effort to stay above the crowd. Therefore, they are rather reluctant to foster other people's careers and usually are not the best team players either. Their motivation can turn into total frustration if they are criticized or confronted with failure. They do not tolerate other heroes around them and are spending a lot of effort to secure their status. Such people tend to produce envy and often disturb the harmony in the organization. Their big ego is often their greatest enemy. Fame is a cost efficient motivator, but as there cannot be too many heroes in a company, it is rather limited to just a few people. Exceptionally talented individuals should be allowed to be heroes if it stimulates their motivation and does not become a burden for the rest of the organization. Controlling their activities is quite difficult, and they require clear guidelines. Establishing a good bonding at a personal level is usually very helpful in handling these people.

The **Business Environment** can be a strong source of motivation, and it may come in different facets.

Many people love their company, and therefore, they are usually very loyal and willing to give their best effort. Their pride about their company may stem from its brand name recognition, its legacy, its vision, its products, or its market position. Even though the statement "I'm proud to work for this company," is often just a stereotype and not always sincere, sometimes it denotes a genuine feeling. As long as the company treats them fairly, these employees are a solid foundation. A difficult situation usually arises when parts of the company are carved out and eventually sold or when businesses are merged into new entities with another identity. In this case, they will usually react extremely disappointed and feel betrayed. Their motivation will drop to zero, and they will use all their energy to impair the carve-out or merger process. People in charge of managing such transactions tend to grossly underestimate this human factor.

A good team can also be a positive motivator. Interacting with interesting and talented team members, sharing success and failure, and striving for common goals often inspires people toward great achievements. Most people love working on a good team. People who know each other well and trust each other, for instance because of a common business background or job history, get along with each other much better. Being part of a successful team motivates each one of them and drives them toward excellence. Sometimes, the temptation to take out good people from their teams and assign them to support weaker ones is high. Unprepared, such a move could easily end in a disaster and destroy a good team. People would feel punished for doing a good job, and their motivation would significantly drop. Even though filling holes by opening new ones is in most instances a bad strategy, such moves still could make sense, like for improving the team dynamics or offering people new career opportunities. To succeed, these personnel shifts need to be thoroughly prepared through comprehensive team dialogues. It would be a big mistake simply expecting people to just continue functioning, no matter the circumstances.

Many people love working for their boss. A charismatic and empathic leader succeeding to establish the right chemistry with his or her employees can become the crystallization point of a very motivated team. For this kind of leader, most people would give their best. Primarily, such a situation is very favorable for the business, but it could also turn into a big risk, should the leader leave the company. As many people would be willing to follow their boss, this risk could eventually materialize in losing the entire team. Naturally, such leaders are in the main focus of headhunters and are often raided by competition.

In the same way as a stimulating environment can strongly motivate people, an inadequate one can demotivate them. This could be the result of an inappropriate management style, bad team dynamics, or incompatible personalities. Persons whose performance suffers under such circumstances should aim at changing their work place.

Geared in the right direction, **Personal Conviction** is the most valuable source of motivation. Unfortunately, it is quite rare. Only a few people are driven by the belief into the values they create and by their intrinsic desire to produce the best possible results. They constantly do a good job because they think it is what they owe to the company and to themselves. They draw their professional satisfaction from the results of their work. These people tend to be rather moderate in their expectations toward the company. Even though being the most valuable company employees, because they usually keep a low profile, it often happens that they do not receive enough recognition and sometimes are even forgotten.

Putting these four motivation categories in correlation with the concrete individual professional output of people reveals a couple of interesting combinations. For the purpose of this analysis, professional output will be categorized as in the following:

Poor: The output of these individuals is below company expectations. Possible reasons could be job requirements exceeding their capabilities or an inappropriate team mix where they cannot unfold their potential. Unfortunately, some people do a poor job even though they could achieve far better results if they just wanted to.

Solid: The contribution of these individuals is according to the standard set by the company. They usually have a good sense of how much professional output they owe to the company in return for their pay.

Excellent: The professional output of these individuals exceeds company expectations. It often also goes beyond their monetary compensation and beyond their job role. Sometimes, companies take these results for granted expecting that they are constantly exceeded. This would be wrong, because it could easily kill motivation.

People of the combination **Poor/Conviction** voluntarily produce only just as much result as required to be still tolerated by the company. They are fully aware that their output is not adequate and deliberately abuse the situation that sub-standard contribution is still accepted. They make life easy for themselves, very often at the expense of their colleagues. Pretending to need support, they let other people do their work. Their level of expertise is rather low, but instead of working to improve their deficiencies, they rather try to hide them. It would be a big mistake to consider these people dumb. To the contrary, they develop smart strategies to protect themselves. Confronted with the truth, they play a victim's role, a victim of circumstances, of not being understood, of too much workload, of mobbing, or of an unfair boss. Eventual disputes with the company often end up in court and unfortunately in many cases with the better end for themselves. These people not only damage the company in terms of their low added value but also in terms of the extra effort required from the part of the organization dealing with them.

Prevention is the only adequate strategy to ensure that such people do not even find their way into the company. It is essential to look for early signs of such behavior in a person's professional track record and during recruiting interviews. Any doubts and inconsistencies need to be clarified latest during the trial period. As extreme situations usually amplify people's strengths but also their weaknesses, exerting occasional pressure during this period is generally a good method to reveal early enough a person's true core.

At the opposite end, the combination **Excellent/Conviction** is what companies should be looking for. These people demonstrate an outstanding performance because it is in their nature. Not achieving the best possible results would make them unhappy. They are the best engineers, project managers, or financial specialists a company can find. They are the pioneers opening new ways, and they are the ones who make the difference in difficult situations. They do not work for rewards or for their boss or for fame. Instead, it is the professional challenge that is driving them. They are ready to tackle difficult tasks, willing to do whatever is necessary, provided that the endeavor makes sense to them. Because they usually take failure personally, they will clearly address potential obstacles and refuse making foul compromises. If these people say, "It's gonna be tough, but let's give it a try," the chances for getting the job done are high.

Acknowledging their achievements and offering them a long term perspective in the company is a must. Bonding at a personal level and treating them as family members is very important. These people are the most eligible for being promoted. In this regard, it is very important making sure that their chances to perform equally well in their new position are high and that such a promotion is only made with the person's consent. A common mistake is to push people into another job role, just because they have performed well in their current one.

Concerning their pay, the fixed portion of their income should be rather high and the variable one comparatively low. These people just want to work and do not want to spend much effort on calculating their bonus. Honoring special achievements with one-time rewards is something they will appreciate as a recognition for exceptional results.

People of the combination **Solid/Conviction** are the strong foundation of any solid business. Like in the Tour de France bicycle race, a team cannot be made out of champions only. Even if a sufficient number of them could be found, it would still not work. Most top teams have only one champion who can potentially win one of the Tour categories. Left alone, these champions could not win even a single stage. They need the support of the other team members to shelter them against the wind, to supply them with water, and to protect them from the attacks of the other teams. Even though somehow depreciative, the German term 'Wasserträger' (water carriers) describes their role best. They are not supposed to win, and they do not want to win as individuals. They want to win as a team. This is also the way a company must work. These people's professional conviction is to simply do a solid job. They are conscious of owing the company their best effort in return for their pay. Still, taking their good work results for granted without acknowledging their efforts would be wrong. Usually reliable and fair, most of them are good team players. Offering these people a long-term perspective is a good investment into the company's sustainability. Treating them fairly and with respect and giving them the feeling that the company is their professional home will keep them motivated. Their remuneration should follow the same approach as for the Excellent/Conviction combination.

The combination **Excellent/Reward** is quite difficult to handle. Individuals belonging to this category are capable of achieving outstanding results, but their motivation is permanently linked to receiving a stimulus. Being good professionals, they can easily get a job somewhere else. If another company offered them a stronger stimulus, they would probably not hesitate moving to a new place. They will always try their limits. "Look, company xyz just made me an offer, and I can't refrain from thinking about it. What do you think?" is a typical question every manager is occasionally confronted with by one of his or her employees. Under the impression of being indispensable and irreplaceable, they will continue this game forever. Giving in would only be recommendable in tight business situations where personnel alternatives are not available. Employees fitting into this category will constantly look left and right in the organization, fearing that somebody else could be better off. From their superiors, they require quite a lot of management effort.

People who are only willing to deliver excellent results in the expectation of a reward need to feel internal competition. Continuously assessing their value contribution helps calibrating their relevance for the company. Making the advantages of their current employment clear to them will usually release some of the pressure these people make in the direction of their superiors. Appraisal of their work is still required, but it should not be too abundant; otherwise, they will immediately try to cash it in.

The appropriate pay approach is to keep their bonuses rather high in comparison with their fixed salary because it fulfills their permanent expectation to receive a reward.

The most common combination is **Solid/Reward**. Regarding the contribution of these people for the company, most things stated for the Solid/Conviction combination also apply. The big difference is that instead of following their internal motivation, they need a reward to do a solid job. This aspect becomes especially relevant in difficult times when rewards like income increases are not possible. Different from the people driven by their professional conviction, their motivation and work results will drop in such a situation.

People in the category **Excellent/Environment** love the place where they work or their boss or their team. Ideally, all of them.

Keeping the inspiring environment stable as long as possible and preparing for potential changes in due time by engaging into discussions with the entire team is the appropriate strategy. Explaining the reasons for a potential personnel change and asking people for their opinion would increase their level of acceptance.

The combination **Poor/Reward** does not make sense. Why would somebody motivated by rewards do a poor job?

The combinations **Poor/Fear** and **Excellent/Fear** are quite seldom and of lower relevance.

Talking Chemistry

In conclusion, the following personnel strategies are recommended:

➔ Fostering individuals with the combinations Excellent/Conviction, Solid/Conviction and Excellent/Environment

➔ Maintaining individuals with the combinations Solid/Environment, Excellent/Reward and Solid/Reward, by keeping in mind to eventually cater for personnel alternatives early enough

➔ Removing from the organization people with the combinations Poor/Conviction and Poor/Reward

➔ Further assessing people with the following combinations:

Excellent/Fear and Solid/Fear—These are valuable contributors, but fear cannot be a long-term motivator. Sooner or later, they will collapse, or their performance will drop.

Poor/Fear—What is the cause of their fear? If fear was the root cause for their poor results, would they demonstrate a better performance in the absence of it?

Poor/Environment—Is the current environment impairing a better performance? Would a transfer into another team improve things?

Motivation ---------------- Performance	Fear	Reward	Environ- ment	Convic- tion
Excellent	assess	maintain	**foster**	**foster**
Solid	assess	maintain	maintain	maintain
Poor	assess	**remove**	assess	**remove**

Analyzing a company's personnel pool, including managers, and allocating especially the key people and people in key departments to the different above described performance–motivation categories provides valuable information regarding the performance potential, sustainability, and robustness of an organization. Therefore, this method is a useful instrument supporting managers in developing the best suitable personnel strategies.

Talking Chemistry

The Pentagon Profile

Managing a business is a complex task. Most people associate managing with just different management styles, such as collaborative vs. autocratic. Reducing the complexity of this job to simply different management styles is too shortsighted. Establishing a comprehensive and meaningful manager profile requires analyzing his or her attitude in relation to a broader spectrum of business-related aspects. Five of them have a decisive relevance in this regard: the manager's attitude toward the business, toward the employees, toward peers, toward superiors, and finally toward himself or herself.

The attitude toward the **BUSINESS** is the most important. In this regard, there are two basic types of managers.

Managers who perceive themselves as the servants of their business want to be genuine *contributors* to the value of the company. As such, their decisions and actions are directed to ensure the long-term success and sustainability of the business. They tend to stay in one management position long enough to assume long-term responsibility and to shape the business according to their professional belief. Without obstructing change if they see a need for it, their decisions will be rather conservative and geared toward not exposing the company to incalculable risks.

At the opposite end, there are managers who regard the business as a means to fulfill their personal career goals. Their actions are mainly aimed at giving their own person maximum positive exposure and therefore toward achieving fast results. As they usually do not stay in one position long enough to be confronted with the long-term consequences of their actions, their concern for the sustainability of the business is generally low. They are ready to take risks if they see a chance for realizing a quick win. Immediate success gives them an aura of champions. Once they are able to cash-in their first successes, they will concentrate on changing into a higher position. With this tactic, they often succeed to zigzag their way up to the top of companies. Calling these managers **opportunists** seems appropriate. Their exhibitionist presentation of pretended exceptional work results combined with their usually charismatic appearance often obscures the overall predatory impact of opportunists on companies.

Contributors are very much concerned about their legacy. If they move to another assignment, they put a lot of effort into preparing this change. Contributors want to leave behind a healthy business and to enable their successors a good start into the job. They will try to participate in the selection of their successors and will insist on a realistic schedule for the change, making sure that there is sufficient overlap to hand over the job to the new manager. They will openly inform their successors about potential business risks and opportunities and will give them valuable guidance.

Opportunists do exactly the opposite. Once their move to another position is certain, they soon lose all interest in their old job and focus entirely on the new one. Who follows them is of little importance. If possible, they will try to hide potential risks and will present opportunities as a 'gift' they are generously making to their successors.

How managers regard their **EMPLOYEES** is also of major relevance. Here again, there are two diametrically opposed types of leaders.

Some managers regard their employees as individuals who need to be treated with respect, whose careers need to be fostered, and whose work results must be recognized and appreciated. They feel a genuine obligation toward their people to actively support them in their professional development and to offer them an inspiring work environment in which they can capitalize on their talents. These managers usually involve their people in the decision making process and allow them a high degree of freedom. Under these conditions, employees can develop their creativity and unfold their total potential. These managers see themselves as *coaches* of their people.

Autocrats regard their employees as business assets who just need to function in their jobs. They give orders and do not accept any objections. "Directions are meant to be followed, not to be discussed," is a common phrase an autocrat's employees often hear. Because autocrats generally avoid personal interaction with their employees, they often hide behind their staff departments and a mountain of rules and regulations, 'the compass' they pretend to be giving to their employees.
In some work areas characterized by rather simple and repetitive tasks, this management style may be effective, but in businesses requiring the creative engagement of people, it is completely unsuitable.

In our modern economy, driven by automation and digitalization, simple jobs are increasingly taken over by machines and will eventually disappear. In the future, human engagement in the value creation will occur at a significantly higher intellectual level and thus will require well educated and creative people. Such people want to be recognized as valuable individuals, require their work results to be acknowledged by their superiors, and disagree with being treated like operating resources. Managers who are able to meet their people at a personal level and who can inspire and motivate them toward great accomplishments will be the ones making the difference in the future war for talents. Managers pursuing an autocratic and impersonal management style increasingly represent a serious business liability and will soon become a relic of the old economy.

In larger businesses, value creation often requires the contribution of different units, which need to be well aligned. If the managers of the different departments pursue individual interests rather than collaborate and align their efforts, the final business result will not be optimal. Therefore, the interaction with **PEERS** should not be neglected in the assessment of management qualities. In this regard, the following two very different management attitudes can be observed.

Some managers are capable of interacting at peer level in a collaborative manner, always looking for solutions to the benefit of the global business. They keep possible personal matters off the job and are ready to accept compromises if this serves the common goal. In complex businesses, the ability to compromise with peers and accept them is an important management quality and defines a genuine ***team player.***

Other managers have difficulties accepting other people on the same level. They perceive them as competitors, even in situations when from an organizational standpoint their job roles are clearly distinct and have no overlap. For these individuals, any relationship must be unequivocal, superior or subordinate. Meeting somebody half way makes them feel uneasy. They will try to subordinate other people from the same hierarchy level. If they do not succeed, they want to be at least perceived as the 'primus inter paris'. In other words, they are the *individualists* of the business. In their constant battle for supremacy, they often become personal. These people invest a lot of effort into becoming the darlings of their bosses and into conquering a privileged position. Rather than stepping up to compensate for a colleague's error, these managers will try to capitalize on such circumstances to weaken the other's position and to strengthen their own. Instead of joining efforts with their colleagues to solve a problem, they prefer escalating the matter to their superiors and waste their energy on preparing the better arguments. In strictly hierarchical business structures, such an attitude is not so damaging, but in functional ones, it can poison the entire organization.

For most people working in hierarchically structured organizations, their relationship with their **SUPERIORS** is quite clear. If the boss gives an instruction or overrules a decision, the subordinates should not hold back with their best effort to implement it in the best possible manner; which is principally correct. This simple rule lays the foundation of every hierarchy. Business is no exception. Managers feeling uncomfortable with following instructions or having problems with occasionally accepting having a decision overruled by their superiors are in the wrong place as employees of a company. They should think about starting their own business.

Some managers choose the way of least resistance and blindly follow their bosses' instructions without further reflection. Whatever their superiors say, they convey unfiltered to their subordinates. Hiding behind their boss is another typical behavior of this type of managers. Such a management attitude represents a big waste of a company's creative potential. The business contribution of such **followers** is questionable.

It is in the interest of the business that, if in doubt with regard to certain given directions, people actively approach their superiors and set forth their arguments. Different from the followers described above, they do not just blindly echo their bosses' opinions and rather try to use their own intellect in the interest of the company. If the boss is still persisting with his or her views, they are able to let go of their own ideas and dedicate their entire efforts to follow the given instructions. This kind of manager can be called a true **loyalist**.

Regarding their relationship with their superiors, most people fall into one of the two above mentioned categories. Obviously, an autocratic manager prefers followers, while coaches prefer being surrounded by loyalists.

The third category is rather an exception, but because in certain business situations it can have a high relevance, it should also be mentioned.
Some people always have their own opinion, and many times, it collides with the opinion of their bosses. They are difficult to control and require a high management effort. In a stable business situation in which sustainability and incremental improvement are the main factors of success, such **rebels** can become a business risk. But sometimes, they come up with revolutionary ideas and initiate a disruptive development for the company. They are also the ideal type of people to break up outdated business habits and crusted structures. Therefore, in certain situations, there is a need for them too.

Finally, the managers' **SELF-PERCEPTION**—the way they sees themselves—is also of great importance.

Most leaders are quite fond of themselves. If this conviction goes so far that a manager sees himself in the middle of everything, he or she is a self-centric *egotist*. Because these people are thinking themselves to be perfect and infallible, self-reflection is a widely unknown term for them. Therefore, they are usually trapped inside their habits and cannot develop themselves.
At the other end, there are mangers who understand that they also need to undergo a development and that only constant self-reflection, continuous learning, and self-improvement will make them a better professional. These people will often ask their employees, peers, and superiors for feed-back on how they can improve in their role. It is hard to find a suitable term to describe them. Probably, the term *reflectionists* comes the closest.

In a *polarized representation* of management qualities, the profile of managers who are contributors to their company, coaches of their employees, team players with their peers, loyalists to their boss, and reflectionists to themselves would make a *perfect pentagon*. Obviously, every business having such managers in key positions can consider itself fortunate. Sadly enough, such people are a rare species and therefore hard to find. Even worse, today's business culture in some companies does not really foster this kind of people. Without recognizing their real value, they are frequently considered as fearing a challenge, as lacking authority and self-confidence, and as being not edgy enough. As a result, opportunistic autocrats, who celebrate themselves and are a nightmare for their employees, still make it too often to the top of companies.

Hopefully, the disruptive change in the economy brought upon by digitalization and artificial intelligence will also change the management culture by fostering managers with true qualities.

The CXO Dilemma

A well-balanced partnership between its CEO and its CFO, governed by team spirit and mutual trust, is of paramount importance for the success of any business. If this relationship functions well, it will send positive signals into the entire organization. In contrast, disharmony at its C-level usually represents a big burden and risk for a company.

Few business partnerships at the top of companies are really successful. In fact, most are rather inefficient. There are plenty of reasons why. The main reason is that, even though well documented in theory, in practice there often exists quite a lot of ambiguity among the two managers regarding their roles and their collaboration to the benefit of the company.

The general role understanding is that the CEO makes all business decisions and bears the ultimate responsibility for the business. The CFO's primary job is to ensure the correctness of the financial business statements and the compliance with accounting principles. Positioning the CEO as the one and only responsible for making all relevant business decisions confines all other business entities to the practical implementation of the directions given by him or her. Such a management approach provokes the question "Is a second person needed at the C-level of companies to fulfill the commercial tasks, or would a Head of Accounting also do?" For many, and especially for commercial people, this question may be irritating, but in many companies the latter would be the case. Why have two persons at the top level, if only one is bearing the whole responsibility for the business? This is a question many CEOs ask themselves. On the other hand, many CFOs feel rather uncomfortable in their second-in-command role and aspire toward an equal relevance and exposure as the CEO. This situation is often the source of reciprocal antipathy and of many conflicts between the two protagonists.

As German business culture is generally more inclined toward a collaborative decision making approach, until about the late nineties, in most companies all important business decisions had to be supported by the technical manager as well as by his or her commercial counterpart. This 'Four-Eyes Principle' put the technical and commercial manager of a company at the same level. It proved to be a valuable management instrument, as decisions were the result of a well balanced process with technical and commercial aspects adequately observed.

During the last couple of decades, the management principle making CEOs the one and only responsible for the business was taken over from the Anglo-Saxon and especially from the American business culture and adopted by most German companies.

What are the consequences of this principle in business today?

In technical businesses, it often means that the CFO's job is limited to just correctly aggregating and reporting the business financials. It also means that his or her participation in the decision making process and in developing the business is rather small. Why is it this way? First, because according to the above mentioned segregation of duties, it is not his or her job.

Second, because most CFOs try to strip down any technical business to generic commercial principles without digging in too much into the business content. This could be either because of the lack of time to familiarize themselves with the business or because of the general reluctance of commercial people to get involved in non-financial matters.

Most CEOs concentrate primarily on technical and operational issues, and often the commercial aspects are eluding their attention. These aspects usually become of interest only at the end of each reporting period, when the commercial managers gather the numbers and draw the bottom line.

This situation often leads to a segregation of the business into two silos, the technical and the commercial one, and it usually goes from the top to the bottom of the company. Interaction is rather limited, not going beyond formally imposed information exchange and reporting processes.

If the business does not run well, usually only the CEO is in the line of fire. It is quite surprising how often CFOs step aside in such a situation and leave the CEO exposed. If the business runs smoothly, they will take a step forward and claim part of the credit. If it is not, they will usually limit themselves to their role, denying any responsibility for operational matters.
Sometimes, when CEOs are too tied up in chasing operational problems, it can be observed that some CFOs step into taking over more and more of the CEO's duties, eventually performing the actual management of the business. Usually lacking the in-depth knowledge of the technical aspects, CFOs tend to reduce the business to numbers and financial indicators. As a result, controlling and reporting activities as well as the headcounts in the commercial departments go up without adding

much genuine value to the business. If CFOs intervene in the definition of the company's strategy, decide about the hiring of technical people, or interfere with operational aspects, a dangerous situation my arise and end up in a total loss of control over the business.

In transactional businesses, such as construction or installation, an important and always recurring question is "How much technical risk is acceptable in one particular endeavor, without jeopardizing the entire business?" Answering this question requires considering and balancing a series of technical, commercial, and legal factors. As such, it cannot be answered neither by the CEO nor by the CFO alone. Such kind of decision making is particularly important when strategic projects which are subject to intense competition are in preparation and when engaging into a calculated risk is unavoidable for keeping the winning chances up. In such situations, CEOs and CFOs do not always act as a good team. The lack of interest of some CEOs for commercial matters and the reluctance of most CFOs to get involved in material matters of the business represent a big shortfall in this regard. CEOs might not know how financially resilient the whole business is, and CFOs might not be able to understand and assess the business risks and opportunities related to such a project.

The fastest and most efficient lever to improve this situation is getting CFOs closer to the business. It is a widespread false assumption that CFOs need only superficial technical subject matter knowledge. Any CEO having a commercial partner at his or her side who is eager to learn about the technical and operational aspects of the business can consider himself fortunate. Though, many CEOs have difficulties in accepting that their commercial counterpart could be also interested in these aspects. They perceive this as an interference with their CEO role, not recognizing the tremendous value tech-savvy commercial people can add to the business. In most CEO–CFO partnerships, it is rather unusual for the former to approach a commercial department and ask for financial information. Similarly, most CFOs are reluctant to contact a project team regarding technical aspects. In practice, this means that often technical and commercial aspects are not properly aligned.

Therefore, CEOs should encourage their CFOs to also take interest in the technical aspects of the business. Visiting project sites together or meeting customers can be very useful in this regard. When eventually the CFO asked, "Can we release some of the risk contingencies in this project?" the CEO could answer, "It would be great if you could talk with the project team and get your own picture." This would be an interesting experience for both managers as well as for their technical and commercial subordinates. By pursuing this approach, technical managers and their commercial counterparts can become a strong team, with each of them able to temporarily jump into the other's role. This team spirit would also be a strong signal to the employees, as they could see that the business has <u>one</u> management rather than two managers and that collaboration between technical and commercial people is strongly endorsed. With each of them occasionally interfering with the other one's area of responsibility, incidental clashes are inevitable. The potential irritation caused by sometimes having to ask oneself, "Why is this guy arguing about this? It's not his job!" would be a small price to pay for receiving the support of a smart, knowledgeable, and committed partner. Nevertheless, both managers need to respect each others home turf.

With time, commercial managers can become well acquainted with the fundamental technical aspects of the business. Even though not being able to cover all technical matters in detail, they would be capable of filtering out the technical information they need for their job. For many CEOs, it would be a great relief to be able to afford being absent from the business for a couple of days with somebody around being able to jump in and keep the ship on course. One of the recipes for a successful partnership is to avoid making the partner feel obsolete.

A good partnership between the technical and commercial business managers will automatically foster a good co-operation between the respective departments. This will save the company a huge amount of slack and inefficiency.

Which are the most important cross functional areas which CEOs respectively CFOs need to cover?

For the CFOs it is of highest importance to understand the most critical aspects of the business. Which operational risks are prevailing and where do they stem from? This kind of knowledge is fundamental to link technical with commercial and contractual risks and opportunities. Without this knowledge, the participation of CFOs in the business can be only superficial, hiding behind numbers and (hopefully) staying away from business decisions.

CEOs usually think in terms of individual business transactions. If one particular business endeavor runs well, they are happy and regard it as a confirmation of their CEO capabilities. If it does not, they take it personal. By the way, this is the way it should be. With this strong focus on the business content, CEOs are in danger of losing the global perspective on the overall business. At this point, CFOs can be of great help by providing smart business analyses, for example about the business robustness and about its sensitivity with regard to various factors. On the basis of such information, better decisions can be made, and business planning becomes far more accurate.

Even though formally everybody pretends having one, really successful CEO–CFO partnerships are rather seldom. The greatest threat in this regard is if the two managers start competing with each other. Albeit not mandatory, the following aspects are helpful to prevent such a situation.

The CEO and the CFO are of different age, preferably the former being the more senior person. Such a combination has the advantage of establishing a respectful relationship at personal level from the very beginning and also of inducing a certain tension between Old and New which can be very prolific for the business. A combination of two people of similar age may bear the risk of establishing an unhealthy competitive environment, especially between younger people.

By the time a new CFO is appointed, the CEO was already in his or her function for some time. In this situation, it is easier for the latter to give his or her new partner more freedom to actively participate in the business. Having successfully managed the business for some time should give him or her enough self-confidence to generously deal with initial friction and to give in on certain things.

Both managers possess solid subject matter expertise in their own domain. It would be an error thinking that the professional weakness of one can be compensated by the strength of the other, because they would never establish a respectful and trustful co-operation.

Talking Chemistry

The chemistry between the two managers is compatible. This is a very important aspect. People sharing common interests and liking each other harmonize better—to their own benefit, to the benefit of their employees, and to the benefit of the business. Forcing incompatible persons into a professional marriage usually ends in a disaster. Often, this compatibility factor is not receiving adequate attention when CEOs or CFOs are appointed.

Both managers are eager to learn beyond the traditional boundaries of their roles and understand and respect each others job.

Does this mean that other combinations are bound to fail? Definitely not! Many combinations can work fine, provided that the protagonists are genuinely interested in dedicating their entire efforts to the business. Even though personal interests will always play a role, they should not prevail, as business must come first.

Regardless of age, experience, or job seniority, when CEOs and CFOs embark on heading a business together, they first should align on a common set of management principles to lead the company. Even though they occasionally could act beyond their roles, the segregation of duties between them must be clear. If not, they would be inefficient, as individuals and as a team. Ambiguity in their individual roles would also be very confusing for the rest of the organization.

CEOs and CFOs must take their time in understanding each other's strengths and ways of approaching things. It is of greatest relevance to share the understanding that their roles are about the business, about their employees, and not about themselves. Regular communication is of utmost importance, especially in the beginning of a new partnership. Setting up weekly alignment meetings solely dedicated to the improvement of their co-operation are strongly recommended in this regard. Questions like "Are we on track as a management team?" or "How do our people perceive us?" should be regularly asked and answered. Competing for importance and exposure is wasted effort. The risk of something like this happening is quite high. One possible reason could be the image and role CEOs feel compelled to meet. It could also be the CFO's ambition to prove that he or she would be the better CEO. This is a situation that both need to prevent. The understanding that their individual successes in their respective roles will primarily depend on the way people perceive them as one management team rather than as two self-centric managers shall rule their partnership. A contentious relationship at the top is poison for the business and for the entire organization. It would automatically lead to the formation of two different clusters in the organization, not necessarily sharing the same interests. Each group would concentrate on pleasing its boss. Showing sympathy and appreciation for the other group could put people in jeopardy. Such situations sometimes escalate to the point that the two managers do not even talk with each other and communicate only through their subordinates. For people, such dysfunction between their technical and commercial managers can become a nightmare, draining them of energy and depriving them of a positive working experience.

A good management team is the result of a dedicated and sustained effort and does not happen by itself. Each CEO–CFO partnership needs time to grow and requires a big personal effort and investment by the two protagonists as well as by their people. Therefore, like with every other important investment, such partnerships need to be diligently planned and regularly assessed.

Any management principle has its advantages and its disadvantages. The good thing about the current practice is that it aggregates the whole responsibility for the business at one point—no excuses, no discussions. The bad thing about it is that if applied too strictly, it can easily waste a lot of the creative potential of an organization. But as with all principles, it is the people applying them who are making the difference.

The Family Business

The term Family Business could be an appropriate description for a company where employees and management share a common objective and feel compelled to the same set of ethical standards. Whether it belongs to a real family—in a social sense—is not relevant in this regard. In such a company culture based on empathy and trust and where roles, rules, and procedures are perceived as useful instruments rather than a purpose in itself, people are finding the appropriate business environment to give their best.

Over the last couple of decades, the business culture continuously degraded, and today it is significantly deviating from a Family Business. It is now determined by the simple equation 'work performance for money'. Period. Nothing more. With the monthly paycheck, companies consider their obligations toward their employees as fulfilled. For the company, the employees are just business assets, and for the employees, the company becomes just a utility to fulfill their personal interests.

<<<<< >>>>>

Sometimes, managers complain about their organization. They feel that it is not functioning well and that they cannot get it under control.

In deed, many organizations do not work really well. The different departments do not pull the same string and spend too much time on fighting and blaming each other. Faults which could have been avoided are still happening and endanger business success. Processes, even though thoroughly documented, fail and do not yield the expected results. Frequent management meetings, alignment workshops, motivation camps, and close control loops seem to have no effect.

Even though all formal management aspects are properly addressed, some businesses are still not running smoothly. For example, complex business endeavors with many parties involved are always in danger of things going wrong, and things will definitely go wrong if only formal aspects are relied on. In this kind of business, the human factor is especially of high importance. Therefore, the alignment of the entire organization with a common goal becomes a mission-critical top-management job. Such an alignment is usually hard to achieve because in most organizations people are primarily pursuing their individual goals. Some people want to maximize their income, some want exposure, some a technical challenge, some want power, and some only want to have a comfortable life. Just like not all metals can get magnetized, which means having all individual magnetic fields of the atoms pointing in the same direction, in many organizations an alignment of objectives will not be possible by just applying standard management methods. Regardless of how much 'magnetization' effort is spent by the management on team events, appeals, or incentives, the 'magnetic field', equal to the operational output, generated by the organization will continue to be weak.

The divergence of interests is a great obstacle for organizations to be efficient. People have different needs and different goals. Their actions are primarily geared toward fulfilling their own interests rather than to the fulfillment of business ones.

Here are a couple of examples: Talented young people want to grow fast in their job and develop their career. They want immediate results for themselves and do not necessarily see a reason in supporting long-term company goals. They are ready to take risks because they know they will get a second chance if they fail. If they do not get what they want, they can easily move to another company. People at the zenith of their career think differently. Most of them earn good money, and many of them know that a further career step is rather unlikely. Thus, preserving their current status has the highest priority. For many of them, their seniority in the company is their greatest asset. Knowing that getting a similar job in another company could be difficult, they are spending a great deal of effort on protecting themselves and their position. They will always follow the safe path and avoid situations where they can get exposed.

In complex organizations with many parties engaged in the value chain, such as sales, R&D, solutions, procurement, operations, and service, clear responsibility is hard to assign, and sharp border lines are difficult to define. If things go wrong, everybody will be trying to disclaim their own responsibility by pointing at another party. Sales would eventually claim, "We can't sell because we don't have the right products." R&D could pretend, "We don't have enough budget to develop the kind of products the market requires." Solutions, "The customer requirements can't be met, sales must renegotiate the technical specs." Procurement, "The specifications were not complete." Operations, "The project schedule is too tight." And finally, at the end of the value chain, Service would also play safe, "We were engaged too late." Everybody has a good explanation why they cannot fulfill their jobs properly. In such a situation the only authority above, the head of the company, fights a battle he or she cannot win. He or she will be devoting all of their time and energy in resolving these disputes instead of taking care of business.

It would be a great mistake to assume or hope that things would fix themselves. "Grown-up people should be capable of putting heads together and coming up with a solution." There are many reasons why they do not. First, because in doing so, they would admit to being part of the problem. "Not my problem!" or "Not my job!" are typical syndromes of a bad organizational culture. A while ago, a little picture titled `Winner of the *Not My Job* contest´ was sent back and forth across the internet, amusing many people. It showed a freshly painted white road-side stripe following the exact contour of a fallen branch that was tipping into the road. Clear case, the painters job was just to draw the white line and not to remove the branch. It would be naive to assume that such things do not happen also in real life. For a manager, these situations are extremely difficult to deal with. It is like swimming in a pool of mud, climbing a glass facade, or drilling holes into granite; there is no grip, the effort is huge, and progress is small. No manager can sustain this constant battle for survival long-term. Eventually, he or she will be replaced sooner or later. Another manager comes in, with new turnaround plans, new alignment meetings, new people, new team events, and new consultants, and the story starts all over again. Constantly replacing people in management positions usually does not solve the problem. In complex businesses, the required skill set is often very specific and understanding the internal dynamics of large organizations takes time. Introducing new managers always bears risks. They could try to implement practices and organizational concepts that may have worked well in their previous jobs, even tough they are totally unsuitable for the new business. Frequent reorganizations do not solve the problem either. People with low motivation or poor skills will never perform well, regardless of the organizational setup.

An additional problem of such stressed organizations is high fluctuation and attrition. Sooner or later, good people lose their faith in the company and leave. The champions are raided by the competition, and many solid performers are able to find new jobs somewhere else. At the other end, bad people will continue to stay, and eventually the company will be left with only mediocre, low motivated under-performers, which is the end of the business.

To avoid such a scenario, the CEO must establish a common goal for all his or her key people, when there is still time, when the organization is still composed of a sound personnel mix made up by a couple of champions to drive the business forward and a sufficient number of solid performers as its foundation. The common denominator for all of them must be a common company objective. Even though they will continue to have their own individual preferences, they must be linked together by the genuine interest in the success of the business. To be accepted and shared by everybody, such an objective must include the interests of the business as well as the interests of the employees. Obviously, the business objective is to generate profit and to produce something customers appreciate. The interest of most employees is job satisfaction, adequate pay, and fair treatment. Generally, employees understand and accept that a company must be profitable, as profitability is a mandatory element of economic sustainability. Producing goods which satisfy the customers is also something most employees want. It gives them the feeling of having a purpose and makes them proud. On the other side, business managers must understand that caring about the interests of their employees usually pays off by raising their motivation and by strengthening their commitment toward the company. Therefore, all of the above objectives are compatible and can be incorporated into a strong company mission statement.

Many current management practices fail to achieve this goal. Even though formally expressing their strong commitment to the company, in their hearts, people tick differently. As often regarded by the company as business assets required to achieve a certain business result, employees, including the managers, will in return regard the company as a means to fulfill their personal goals. For some, this personal goal might be a professional challenge; for others, it is the power and exposure a management position can offer; for most, the main goal is simply more money. Seldom, the first interest of employees is to serve the company. Though intriguing, the above statement can be easily sustained. Let us look, for example, at how many top managers leave their company to join the strongest competitor and are using their knowledge to the detriment of their old business. People do not genuinely care about their company, and companies do not care about people. In conclusion, for most people, the company is something abstract and intangible. Therefore, they will not be able to build any sort of emotional bonding with it. For most employees, the question of what the company really means to them would be hard to answer. It would produce the usual stereotype answers like "Proud to be part of a great team," but nothing beyond.

If the CEO regarded his or her company as a Family Business, this would be a totally different approach. In private life, for most people their own home is one of the biggest assets, and they would do anything to protect it. Equally, if they regarded the company as their professional home, they would probably put business interests at the same level with their own ones, eventually even above. Maybe not all people, as it is rather un-realistic to expect that everybody would immediately embrace this attitude. This cultural change is a long-lasting top-down process and must be initiated by the CEO. In a first step, it should be applied to his or her core management team. The coherence and efficiency of this inner circle consisting of maybe ten to fifteen people is mission-critical for the success of the company. Later on, this new culture can be flown down step by step throughout the entire organization.

The Family Business concept has nothing to do with real family relationship, as none of the players must be relatives. To the contrary, such ties would induce other than business-related interests, and therefore, they would not be helpful. It is all about business ownership. Even though they are not the 'de jure' proprietors of the company, people can be encouraged to take on ownership. As the 'family head', the CEO must trans-form his or her management team into a community of inter-ests, totally geared toward the global business success of the company. He or she needs to set the rules. This goes far be-yond establishing formal processes and regulations. It espe-cially means defining how the management team members have to understand each others role and how to treat each other. It also means defining success or failure from a team perspective and specifying how individual accountability is to be understood in the global business context. The CEO must make clear that he or she takes individual performance for granted and that real service for the company starts when people co-operate to solve problems also outside their own silo of direct responsibility. The CEO must also assure his or her reports that it is his or her role to protect them, to foster their careers, and to create an appropriate business environment where they can capitalize best on their strengths. The glue keeping this circle together is mutual trust. The trust of their employees is nothing managers can win easily. Some try to generate trust by organizing team events, workshops, and other types of meetings. This will not work, because in these gatherings, people are not being genuine and are just playing a role. Trust must be earned day by day, and it takes a lot of time and personal investment.

One of the opportunities where managers can start earning trust is the target setting process. Facing their direct reports with unrealistic business targets is one of the biggest sources for distrust. Defining challenging but still achievable targets together with their teams and sustaining and defending these targets in discussions with their superiors is what managers should do. Instead, many agree to being dictated absurd goals from their superiors and blindly pass them on to their subordinates. When such false expectations fail to materialize at the end of the year, it leaves behind frustrated and demotivated people feeling betrayed and abused by their managers.

Making false promises to one's own employees is another dead-proof method for destroying trust. For a manager, it could be quite tempting to promise people something like a salary raise or a promotion if they agreed to take over an unpleasant job. This is acceptable if such promises are kept. But too many times, such promises do not materialize. Sometimes, because the manager simply forgets about them or because he or she tries to avoid the effort required to fulfill them. Sometimes, simply because conditions have changed. And frequently, because in the meanwhile another manager has taken his or her position, and the new person does not feel any obligation with regard to promises made by his or her predecessor. In any case, the employees will feel betrayed and lose their trust in their managers and the company. Employees make false promises too, such as by agreeing to business targets they cannot achieve or by proposing technical solutions they cannot implement, which are a good reasons for earning the distrust of their managers.

Sometimes, distrust between managers and their subordinates takes strange forms. Some managers want everything and preferably at once. They want big orders and high profits, but they are not prepared to take risks. Especially in larger organizations, the reluctance to accept business risks is a widespread phenomenon. Nobody wants to get exposed, and many people prefer losing a business opportunity rather than taking risks. This risk phobia often stems from not understanding the business well enough and from being surrounded by incapable or untrustworthy people. If these two aspects come together, they mutually amplify each other. Driven mainly by the fear of making mistakes, managers who do not understand the business well enough or are surrounded by incapable people sometimes do strange things. To protect themselves, some are asking their subordinates to personally 'guarantee' the success of a business transaction—"I am making you personally accountable." Such bizarre practices are nonsense for several reasons. First, because all personal matters must be kept out of the business. Capable persons would simply act responsibly with all due diligence and do their best to ensure the success of a business endeavor, as part of their job. Why would they have to personally guarantee that they were doing their job. Without understanding what they do, incapable people would anyway guarantee anything. Second, such a guarantee would have no value. What could the managers do with it? Go to their boss and exculpate themselves by pointing at their employees? Hiding behind their own people in front of their superiors would be equal to disclaiming their own role. Furthermore, such an attitude would be professionally deeply unethical. And third, because such practices are poisoning the organization by allowing suspicion, fear, and distrust to rule the business. All things, dedicated and responsible managers would stay far away from.

Capable of balancing risk and opportunity, knowledgeable managers will support their people in the decision making process. By making their experience available, they can significantly help improve the business maturity of their organizations. On the other hand, strong organizations can support new managers in familiarizing them with a new business, provided that they are willing to learn and to adapt to the new situation.

Formal rules and regulations are necessary and should generally govern the business. They are the result of the experiences an organization has gathered over the years and are an important instrument for assuring business consistency and for enabling improvement. They are also an essential prerequisite in making sure that business matters are treated with all care. Though, rules and regulations alone cannot guarantee business efficiency. Many managers fail to understand this fact and blindly rely on them by ignoring the human factor, which plays an even more important role. Even though required, rules can also represent a danger. Especially when they replace common sense. Ignoring that it may jeopardize an important business objective, people sometimes continue to blindly apply them by the book just to not expose themselves.

In a Family Business, the CEO must make clear that he or she expects exactly the opposite from his or her managers. He or she would give them the freedom to eventually deviate from the rule book to support a business goal, provided that they are able to sustain their decisions and that they are not crossing certain lines. Sometimes, an 'out of the box' decision is required to ensure the success of a business transaction, and people should not be afraid to make it. CEOs must assure their managers that they would always respect their decisions, as long as they serve the business. They should also make clear that they would always stand by their people and that this would also be the case if they made mistakes. In a complex business, failures cannot be totally ruled out, regardless of how thorough people are and how precisely processes are followed. In a Family Business failure would embarrass people and disappoint them primarily about themselves. Genuine disappointment about their own bad performance is a far better motivator than the fear of consequences.

Only a few managers have the capability of becoming 'family heads'. The required skills are not taught during professional education and cannot be acquired in seminars either. A good foundation for a successful management career is built during early education when terms like respect and fairness are set. These values maintain their validity also throughout professional life. The rest is training on the job, learning from good and also from bad examples, and, most important, constant self-reflection about one's own management style. Self-confidence is another important ingredient. To be self-confident, a person must have something special to offer. The best thing a CEO can offer is a good vision and the ability to motivate people for committing to make it happen. This self-confidence must be an intrinsic part of the person and not just an acted attitude. It takes time to build. Many top managers are just playing a role in their function. Instead of being genuine, they start in a new position by following a list of do's and don'ts. Who really cares what new managers have accomplished in their first 100 days? Unless, one of their objectives was winning the trust of their employees. Very few managers spend enough time and effort to get into the heads of their people. In a Family Business, the CEO needs to know what is on the minds of his or her management team members, what is driving them, what their personal expectations are, and what they are expecting from him or from her. This profound understanding of each other requires a lot of interaction at personal level and building of trust. One can only trust a person one knows. During this process, the CEO must come to know which people he or she can trust and which he or she can only rely on, which is not the same. One can only trust reliable people, but not all reliable people can be trusted. One can rely on people for executing a specific task to the best of their knowledge and to the extent of their capabilities. Trusting people that even in a difficult situation their decisions will still be governed by the interests of the company is something different. Delivering a sealed envelope containing an important confidential document requires a reliable person. Letting somebody seal the envelope and deliver it requires a trusted one.

Unlike in a real family, in a Family Business the manager can still choose which members he or she accepts for the company's inner circle, and only trusted people should find their way in.

It could be assumed that offering generous incentives would be a good method of fostering the sense of business ownership of people. This assumption is wrong. People usually take incentives for granted shortly after and regard them as a regular component of their income, something the company owes them. When eventually an incentive is lower than expected, people are disappointed and feel punished.

Ownership starts when people genuinely feel an obligation to make their best possible contribution to the company and when they understand that the overall business success is directly linked to their decisions and actions. Encouraging people to make decisions and respecting their decisions is a strong instrument for generating trust and ownership. It is the CEO's responsibility to build an appropriate decision making culture in his or her company with clear definition of individual business mandates and areas of responsibility. Many managers are reluctant to make decisions and prefer reducing their role to the participation in the decision making. Delegating the responsibility for making important decisions to the level above is a widespread awful habit. Managers should understand that making decisions is an intrinsic part of their job and that with every decision they make, they also take personal responsibility for the related outcome.

Some types of organizations make it quite difficult for people to assume responsibility for their decisions. As mentioned earlier, in functional ones, responsibility is diluted because nobody except the CEO is accountable for the overall result and because the decisions of the different departments do not necessarily converge in the direction of the total business. Such a setup could work in small and rather simple businesses, but it often fails in more diverse and complex ones. A divisional structure makes it much easier to delegate responsibility. Divisional heads have the global responsibility for a certain type of business. They should have all the critical resources they need for their business under their control. The CEO's engagement in the decision making process regarding the operational business should be kept at a minimum. It should occur only in the case of especially critical transactions and global company issues or at request of the divisional managers if they need support.

A figurative description of certain management styles can be made by using an analogy with foosball. Some managers run their organizations like foosball players. The manger controls all handlebars and all players at any time. Only he or she is responsible for all moves and thus for the result at the end of the game. All his or her players are just utilities. Which talented professional would like to be part of such a game in real life? The opposite would be teaching his or her players the rules of the game, making clear what his or her expectations are, and letting them play. To the outside, he or she would still be responsible for the final result, but inside the organization the perception of personal responsibility and business ownership would be totally different. Such a business environment would definitely be far more attractive for good people.

As 'family heads', the CEOs would give their company a new face. They would change the abstract and intangible image of the company and give it a human touch. They would make the company something people can identify with and where they feel being active part of a greater success story. Something they really care about and for what they would be determined to give their very best without necessarily expecting an immediate reward. Something they could call their professional home. Something that could be called a Family Business.

Closing Words

In its core sense, managing means leading people. Fostering the development of the employees for their own benefit and for the benefit of the business is the most rewarding aspect of leading. Many managers confound leading with ruling over people. They move people around like figures on the chess board, where each figure has a special capability and is supposed to do something specific. Chess champions are capable of smartly anticipating their opponents' moves and of developing the most ingenious strategies to win the game. They are wisely managing their chessmen, knowing when it is time to sacrifice the one or the other or to make an exchange. Still, would anybody automatically call such chess champions good managers or even leaders? Probably not. Would such exceptional skills make a good manager and leader? Not necessarily, but they would certainly help. Chessmen are static and cannot develop additional skills. They are totally predictable. Other than its first move, the pawn can only take one step forward, and the rook can only run along a straight line. Unlike the figures on a chess board, people change. Their character, their beliefs, their behavior, and motivation are shaped and influenced to a great extent by their working environment. Good leaders are capable of creating a positive business culture, inspiring and motivating people to develop their skills and to achieve their best possible business performance. Trust and respect are the most relevant elements of the foundation of leadership. Without them, any effort in this regard is bound to fail. Sadly enough, in many organizations trust and respect are replaced by fear and authority. There are several reasons for this deplorable situation. It starts with the fact that learning to respect others has increasingly lost its relevance in the education of people. With individual self-fulfillment becoming their principal goal, people have gradually dumped reciprocity and respect as useless ballast. Treating people respectfully requires extra effort. Generally, people have a respectful attitude toward their superiors. But this is more out of necessity rather than an intrinsic quality, as most of them fail to demonstrate the same attitude toward peers or subordinates. In the absence of mutual respect, trust is impossible to build. Nobody can genuinely trust people without respecting them. As already addressed earlier in this book, mutual trust does not happen automatically. It must be earned, and it requires a big effort, from the managers as well from their employees.

From a manager's perspective, fear and authority are far easier to handle. Authority is usually a given as a result of a person's position in the organizational hierarchy. Spreading fear from a position of authority does not require much effort, and it does not require any special skills either. Therefore, the less talented managers are, the more likely fear and authority will become the main instruments in their managerial repertoire.

It is surprising that even in our modern economies, most people are still getting blinded by authority and perceive fear as an intrinsic emotion in relation to it. As a result, managers who celebrate their authority and use it purposely to establish a culture of fear and subordination in their organizations are often regarded as strong and with aplomb. As they often make their way up into the top positions of businesses, this ignorant and disrespectful management style is perpetuated and has infested many organizations.

Talking Chemistry

If it is so easy to rule by authority and fear, why would anybody starting in a management position make the extra investment and spend the extra effort to pursue a career path based
on respect and trust?

My answer to this question is the long-term dividend such a
management approach yields, both in terms of personal satisfaction and business success. The pay-back of people who are
trusted and treated with respect, who are encouraged to contribute with their own ideas, and who have the freedom to
grow in their jobs is enormous. The greatest reward managers
can expect from their people is the acknowledgment that they
deserve their position and that they are the right persons to
lead their employees. For the business, the long-term dividend
of trusting employees and of treating them with respect mate-
rializes in terms of less personnel fluctuation, higher productiv-
ity, better product quality, and as a result superior business
performance. But there are also significant soft benefits a positive business culture can generate for the company. It sup-
ports its good reputation, it attracts new champions and re-
tains talent.

Mangers shying away from embracing an approach based on
respect and trust are wasting the chance for an accomplished
career. Sooner or later, they will vanish, and the only emotion
they leave behind is relief.

Those going the extra mile to dedicate themselves not only to
the business but also to their employees can become great
leaders and part of the company's legacy.

The expected economic transformation resulting from the
tremendous technological development and the introduction of

new (hybrid) work models is also likely to change the business culture of companies, making more room for value managers. Winning the race for the best and most talented people requires a new management style in total contrast to conventional approaches based on hierarchies, subordination, and authority.